Hospice Hounds

HOSPICE HOUNDS

Animals and Healing at the Borders of Death

Michelle A. Rivera

Lantern Books • New York
A Division of Booklight Inc.

2001
Lantern Books
One Union Square West, Suite 201
New York, NY 10003

The names given in this book of individual patients in the
hospice, along with some details of their lives, have been
changed to protect their privacy.

Printed in the United States of America

Library of Congress Cataloging-in-Publication Data

Rivera, Michelle A.
  Hospice hounds : animals and healing at the borders of death /
Michelle A. Rivera.
        p. cm.
  ISBN 1-930051-36-0 (pbk. : alk. paper)
    1. Hospice care. 2. Animals—Therapeutic use. 3. Healing—
Miscellanea. I. Title

R726.8. R58 2001
362.1'756—dc21

                                              2001020371

For Katherine and Sable
Together again, having met on the other side

Acknowledgments

I AM TRULY APPRECIATIVE OF MY HUSBAND JOHN for supporting me and enduring my many days and nights away from him so that I could be with my beloved partners, Woody and Katie. If not for his love, I would never have undertaken this project. I also wish to thank Lisa and Michael Berkenblit for sharing their amazing dogs with me, and trusting me to care for their precious canine children as I would my own. Other friends and supporters who were instrumental in the creation of this book are: Adriana Strand, for encouraging me to become a pet therapist in the first place; Marie Hope Davis and the Peggy Adams Animal Rescue League, for understanding that I needed much time and space away from my job as a humane educator so I could write; Dr. Thomas Lipin, for keeping me healthy enough to pursue my passion for working with animals despite severe allergies to them; Fr. Tom Vengayil at St. Jude's Church, for reassuring me that God does, indeed, love animals and wants them to be protected and safe; Marc Bekoff, who walked this journey with me as a mentor and a friend; my precious Tyrone Bob, who stayed by my side the entire time I was writing; and my sons, Jay Michael Rivera and Toby Francis Rivera, for keeping a sense of humor while growing up extraordinarily well despite having a writer for a mother. Thank you all.

Contents

Foreword

Letting dogs love and heal us

IT IS INDEED A TRUE PLEASURE TO WRITE A foreword for *Hospice Hounds*. We should all be in Michelle Rivera's debt for undertaking this very important, timely, personal, and inspirational project. Personal stories are wonderful means for conveying difficult and personal messages, and they can stimulate each and every one of us to reflect on stories that we can share with others, as well as expand our horizons into worlds that we do not now inhabit but just might in the future.

In November 2000 I met Michelle in a coffee house in Coral Springs, Florida, when visiting my own parents, one of whom (my father at eighty-three) is vibrant and healthy and one of whom (my mother at eighty) suffers serious cognitive and physical decline. This up-close-and-personal meeting with Michelle allowed me to see the fire and radiance in her eyes—her deep and selfless conviction that this, her very first book, was going to be an important work that would make people think and re-think their interrelationships and interconnectedness with dogs. She is right.

Hospice Hounds is packed with stories that will calm you, make you dig deeply into your heart and soul, and likely bring tears to your eyes. These tales will pull you out of your own misery and enable you to share in and empathize with other's misfortunes. Sometimes this is what it takes to make strides in the care of terminally ill people (and the world at large), and, as you will see, dogs (and cats and other animals) are a natural prescription for sharing their goodwill and unconditional love in a hospice, given their long historical and reciprocal association with humans. These animals are safe and non-threatening beings who offer much spirit and deep souls, even to people who previously did not like them or think much about them.

Hospice Hounds begins with Michelle telling the deeply personal story of her own mother Katherine's illness and her dying appeal to have the company of a dog. On her deathbed, Katherine pleaded, "I need to see a dog. I need a wagging tail." Circumstances were such, however, that there was no family dog at the time. Katherine did not live with a dog because she had been living in a senior citizen complex that did not allow dogs. Katherine had moved in with Michelle when she became terminal, but Michelle and her family were also living without a dog because they did not have the time to care properly for a companion animal during their busy days and nights. Eventually, Michelle quit her job to stay home and take care of Katherine so the time was right to bring a dog into their lives. Tyrone joined the family and was there when her mother died, along with Sable, Michelle's cat. These two loving buddies, two "healers with fur coats," lay on the bed beside Katherine.

I know of these silly and archaic rules that exclude animals from hospices and housing complexes only too well. Once, while visiting my parents, my father called his friend, Ginger, whose husband had recently died, so that she could show me her new treasure, a teacup poodle, not surprisingly named Tiny, whom she carried inside her shirt! Tiny, whom Ginger pampered and deeply loved and who also pampered and deeply loved Ginger, brought Ginger much joy in the absence of her husband. But, because of the rules of the house imposed by the homeowner's association, dogs were not allowed on the premises. I can guarantee you that this wonderful small dog was much less of a nuisance then most of Ginger's human neighbors. Yet Ginger had to move because dogs were banned. What was very interesting to me was that my mother, who had been bitten by a dog when she was young and feared dogs throughout her life, also found Tiny to be a welcome and comforting friend. She actually let Tiny lay on her lap and smiled from ear to ear as Tiny burrowed into her blanket and heart.

Why is this so? Why are dogs such good healers? One answer might be that when we allow dogs into our lives they readily ignite and awaken our senses, spirits, and souls. They, and many other animal beings, offer us raw, naked, unfiltered, and unconditional respect, humility, compassion, trust, and love. They are not social parasites who prey deceitfully and selfishly on our good will as some popular writers would want you to believe. Rather, as Michelle and others poignantly point out, dogs are our true friends—with whom we are tightly bonded and involved in a sort of mutual admiration society (see for example, Alan Beck and Aaron Katcher's book, *Between Pets and People: The Importance of Animal Companionship*; see also www.vet.purdue.edu/depts/vad/cae/).

I hope that *Hospice Hounds* is read widely and that its many important messages make a difference for those unfortunate human beings who are suffering in their last days of life, as well as their devoted caretakers who want the best for their beloved friends and family members. Dogs are "intuitive therapists." They truly want to make us feel better, to heal us, and we are remiss for not allowing them to do so, to be our best friends. We are depriving them of following their natural instincts. I imagine that it is likely that as we allow dogs to do what they do best, comforting us in difficult times, we will discover even additional mutual benefits from their unconditional giving. I feel certain that the give-and-take that characterizes dog–human interactions will blossom into even more meaningful and deep interrelationships.

Bless you, Michelle, for undertaking this project, for being selflessly generous in sharing your own pains, and for a producing a book that will make a difference to so many human beings and their canine companions.

Marc Bekoff *lives with his dog companion, Jethro. He is Professor of Biology at the University of Colorado, Boulder. Bekoff is author or editor of 13 books including the* Encyclopedia of Animal Rights and Animal Welfare, The Smile of a Dolphin: Remarkable Accounts of Animal Emotions, *and* Strolling with Our Kin: Speaking for and Respecting Voiceless Animals. *He and Jane Goodall have recently co-founded Ethologists for the Ethical Treatment of Animals (www.ethologicalethics.org).*

Introduction

THE DOGS YOU WILL READ ABOUT IN THESE stories are my kids. I am thankful to and proud of them for being the kind and gentle beings they are, and for being able to translate that kindness and gentleness into an ability to bring comfort to the terminally ill. They are fantastic beings in their ability to adapt to and maintain their calm and confident selves in so many different situations. They go into a television studio every week, they visit rambunctious children at schools, they come to work in our veterinary hospital every day, and, maybe most importantly, they make hospice visits.

I was introduced to pet facilitated therapy while in veterinary school, where I also became involved with the Delta society. I have been reading the society's journal *Anthrozoos* for many years, and have been fascinated with its articles pertaining to the effects of companion animals on people. I have witnessed the profound effects they have on people on a daily basis in my work. I have also seen it at the personal level—the effect our companion animals have on my infant daughter has been a joy. My daughter Emma's first word was "Kelly," the name of our cat. Her first concern every morning in her crib is where her dogs and cats are. One of my most cherished memories is that of my beloved Grandmother Ida, who toward the end of her wonderful life began to fade mentally. It was almost impossible to engage her through the haze of senility. What it took to be able to connect with Ida, to see her lucid once again, was the mere mention of pets. This is a memory my entire family cherishes. The extraordinary rapport between pets, infants, and the aged makes me realize the bond we have with these animals is deep within us. It is a testament to how deeply and basically we are intertwined.

Michael Berkenblit graduated from the University of California in 1986. He is co-owner of Village Animal Clinic, North Palm Beach, Florida with his wife Melissa Degen, DVM ACVIM. He has been actively involved with Delta Society since 1983 when he won a Delta Society scholarship. Dr. Berkenblit serves on several committees oriented towards educating children about humane animal interactions, and he is the Canine Companions for Independence veterinarian in his area.

1

Bring me a dog...

There is no being more supportive
than a friendly dog

KATHERINE LAY IN THE BED WEEPING. HER SAD face was turned toward me and she held the metal bedrail with both hands, struggling to stay on her side so she could see me. She was so small that she had to peek through the rails, and she was pleading. "Bring me a nice dog, " she begged through tormented tears, "Why isn't there a dog here? I *need* to see a dog. I *need* a wagging tail. Can't you find me a nice dog?" Her urgent appeal tore at my heart. This was my dying mother, and I was unable to grant this most simple of requests.

With cancer, the magic number is five. If a patient can survive five years after a cancer diagnosis, conventional wisdom holds that he or she has it beat. But the luck of the Irish and all the incense and Catholic rituals in the world could not save my mother. She died four years and eleven months after "beating" breast cancer. I was her sole caregiver, and her disease escorted us into the restless and confusing world of medicine—a world that demands we leave our familiar places, and where questions bring more questions.

My mother learned her battle with breast cancer was a lost cause on a bright Florida Christmas Day in 1991. A stroke had killed my father nine years earlier, ending a forty-two-year marriage that Mom liked to refer to as "oak and ivy." She was living alone in a small senior-citizen complex when the cancer we thought was a vile memory returned like a stalker triumphantly trapping his terrified victim.

In my sleep, I heard the distant sound of a phone ringing. It was a little past 6:00 am. My husband John was sleeping peacefully by my side. Our sons Jay and Toby (having passed the age of arising at dawn to see what Santa left) were asleep in their rooms, too. My mother's voice on the phone was weak. "Mike," she said, calling me by her pet name for me. "I can't move. I fell trying to get out of bed and I just don't have strength in my arms to get up." She had been lying there for two hours, waiting for a "more reasonable" time to call me. When I got to her apartment I found her on the floor next to her bed. The mattress was stripped bare and the bedclothes pooled around her. In attempting to use them to pull herself up, she had succeeded only in pulling them down around her. Her right arm had been weakened by a radical mastectomy almost five years before, and she couldn't lift herself off the floor.

And there was something much more sinister. She complained of a terrible pain radiating down her arm that seemed to be coming from her back. She was in agony and it took all the strength I had to get her up and into the car. The emergency room doctor was solemn as he read the radiographs. He confirmed that the cancer had returned to stake a claim in her spine. We had almost made it to the magic five-year point. Almost.

When a doctor determines a patient is in the end state of a terminal illness, the focus shifts to preparing the patient for death, and keeping her physically and spiritually comfortable. The idea behind hospice is that patients die with dignity. Patients have to be referred by their doctors, the criteria being that they have a life-limiting illness that will end their life in three months or less. In my mother's case, the oncologist made the necessary referral, and Mom and I paid a visit to the nearest hospice, a center in sunny South Florida.

Upon entering the center we found a beautiful atrium with a high ceiling and massive skylights. In the center of the atrium was a marble pond and fountain, and encircling the atrium were gigantic palm trees, lush foliage, and colorful tropical flowers. On a side wall stood an enormous aquarium with colorful fishes and brilliant coral plant life. There were benches around the pond and under the trees, allowing visitors to sit in an atmosphere of pure beauty and serenity.

A friendly administrator greeted us and made a point of introducing us to every employee and volunteer as we made our way around the facility. We were shown into an unoccupied patient room. The rooms were all similar and each had a private bath, a bed, two armchairs, a table, a nightstand, and a loveseat-sized sofa bed. Sliding glass doors opened onto a private patio with a pretty little tropical garden. Family members could sleep overnight on the sofa bed, or spend the day watching the television mounted on the wall. There were several brightly lit lobbies where family members could read, play cards, work puzzles, and visit. And family members are not restricted only to humans. Every member of the family was welcome to come spend precious time with their dying loved one. There was also a tiny chapel, cool and dark, with deep rich hunter-green carpeting, heavy wooden benches, and a simple altar for impromptu memorial services. Down the hall from the chapel was a small cafeteria.

A patient who has a friend or family member to care for them may elect to stay at home, and hospice supports these patients too. Hospice arranges for the delivery and set-up of a hospital bed and a visiting nurse as well as medications. With all this available support, we decided we would keep Mom at home. Toby, our younger child, took to sleeping on the couch and his bedroom was turned into a hospital room.

The day my mother cried for a dog was soon after moving in with us. I was doing dishes in the kitchen when I heard a soft moaning coming from her bedroom. I turned the water off and stood silently, waiting to see if I heard it again. I did. I went to the bedroom and stood at the door a moment, watching my mother from the doorway. She was lying in the bed, her hands on the side rail. Her hair, once champagne blonde, had gone thin and white, and her naturally rosy face had turned ashen. She looked at me with cloudy blue eyes.

"Miiiike." She drew my name out like it was a mantra. "Miiiike. I need a dog. Why don't you have a dog?" she demanded. She was right. I didn't have a dog. John and I had been working long hours a day before I had taken this leave of absence. The boys were involved with school and sports. Sadly, we just didn't have enough time to devote to caring for a dog. Not having a dog created a terrible void in our family, but we were realistic—we had Sable, a Siamese cat, and I called for her now. She appeared at my side, rubbing my legs and meowing the distinctive Siamese yowl. I gently lifted her and placed her by my mother's side on the bed.

"Look, Mom," I said. "We have this lovely cat." Sable settled in gratefully, happy to have the warm softness of a reclining body to snuggle against. She was always available to join in as a nap partner. She looked up at me with sleepy blue eyes and began to purr. Mom absently stroked her for a moment. "Thank you for saying that we have this lovely cat. She is a lovely cat. But I want a dog." Like a toddler's mother who knows her stubborn child is gearing up for an impressive whine session, I knew that this was not to be an easy fix. "Please get me a dog. I need a dog. I love dogs," she pleaded again. Then she became angry. "Why don't you have a dog?" she demanded. "How can anyone not have a dog?"

The short answer of why my mother didn't have a dog was because of the rules in the senior citizen complex in which she lived. Yet, here was my dying mother, asking me for the one thing that I could not produce, a dog. It could have been the medicine that made her so insistent, or maybe even the disease process. Maybe it was a combination of both that made her so unreasonable. But her request was from the heart, and as she continued to insist I bring her a dog, her voice became louder. I was in for a hissy fit, I just knew it, and I had to think quickly.

It was the middle of the day and most of our neighbors were at work. Where in the world would I find an instant dog? I thought. I considered my options. Terry across the street would be home. She had Kodi, a chow-chow. But Kodi was cranky and had recently bitten Terry's own mother in the face for refilling his water dish when he was eating. No, I didn't think Kodi would work. Who else? There was Becky. She had two dogs and lived three houses down from me, but Becky was at work. I was vaguely aware of a dog across the street from Becky. I knew the family enough to say hello and chat about the weather. The Johnson family had moved from New York as I had, and knew, as did all the neighbors, that I was caring for my dying mother.

My mother was crying now. "A nice dog! I really want to see a nice dog before I die. Is that too much to ask?" She was getting a little dramatic and pulling out all the stops. I was desperate. I looked out the window and saw Marion Johnson's car in her driveway. I told Mom to hold on and ran down the street to Marion's house. I was relieved when I heard a dog barking at my knock, and even more so when Marion answered the door. Marion was a friendly lady and she smiled when she saw me. Seeing the look on my face, she asked what was wrong.

"Marion," I said, knowing that my request would sound bizarre. "I need to borrow Buddy for a while." Naturally, she looked confused. I quickly explained my situation, which sounded ridiculous in spite of the grim circumstances. Marion immediately understood and left to get Buddy's lead. Buddy was happy to see the lead in her hand and wagged his tail in delight.

Our family loved big dogs. My sister Kerry bred Newfoundlands, and my father was a New York State trooper who worked with bloodhounds. When I was born, we had a bull mastiff/great Dane mix named for the patron saint of policemen, St. Michael the Archangel. We called him Mike. When we moved to Florida while I was still in high school, my parents bribed me with my choice of a dog because I was resentful at having to move from my school and friends. We looked through the shelter but couldn't find a big dog I wanted. We knew Kerry's Newfoundlands were not a good choice for South Florida.

So, my indulgent parents, guilt-ridden at a circumstance beyond their control, gave me a dog encyclopedia as a gift. I looked through the wonderful picture book and decided on a beagle. "Oh please," said my mother as she made a face. "You can pick something a little more singular than that, can't you? I mean, a beagle is so common, and they aren't very bright. And we need a big dog, really. We can't have a little dog like a beagle. Don't you want a nice great Dane or mastiff? Really, pick something else dear." My mother the society type had spoken. We ended up with a neurotic Irish Water Spaniel named Patrick.

This memory came surging back at me as I placed Buddy, a thirteen-year-old overfed *beagle* before my mother. "Look, Mom," I said much too cheerfully. "Buddy's come to see you." Sable practically rolled her eyes at the sight of this fat, silly beagle, and the look my mother gave me clearly told me that I had to be kidding.

"Oh well, I think I will take a nap now," she declared, without so much as a nod to Buddy. With that, Marion, Buddy, and I were abruptly dismissed.

We all know the feeling that "someday," we'll laugh about a situation. But we laughed about that situation *that day*. That Irish humor got us through the last days of my mother's life. The next day, after much soul-searching and family discussion, we decided it was time to bring a dog into our family. I was home now for an indefinite time; we had time to raise a puppy. Yes. Now was the right time.

A week later John answered an advertisement in the paper and brought home the perfect puppy, whom we named Tyrone for a county in Northern Ireland and a small town in upstate New York close to where Mom grew up. He was a three-month-old standard poodle with curls as black as onyx. I placed him in Mom's bed and she immediately took him into her arms and fondled his soft floppy ears. The two of them lay together like that for hours. My mother became noticeably less anxious. She talked to him way into the night. She told him the stories her mother used to tell her: stories of Dublin, the Kerry dancers, and the legacy of her ancestors, the Downs of County Claire. She whispered into his ear that she feared her imminent journey, yet longed to be with her husband. Never far from her side, Tyrone wagged his tail happily at her stories, and snuggled even closer to her tortured body. Sable, the night nurse, had another healer with whom to share the awesome task of comforting a dying mother.

One day, I answered the phone. It was Mom's old friend, Edith. I handed Mom the phone and waited a moment. She seemed to be waiting for me to leave, so I did. Still petting Tyrone's head, I heard her whisper excitedly into the phone. "Edith, you know how I have always been so fond of baby goats? Well, they got one! Yes, they did and they put him in my bed." Tipsy with drugs, she had confused a puppy with a baby goat. And once again, we laughed at the incongruity of it all.

Having Tyrone in our lives at that time was therapy for all of us. Every morning, I had nothing to look forward to but the possibility that this could be the day my mother died. Nothing I did, no matter how sacrificial, heroic, or well-meaning could save her life now. But Tyrone brought me something life-affirming, something to look forward to, a project on which to refocus. The housetraining, the socialization, the puppy vaccines; all of it served to take my mind off my troubles and focus on something living, positive, and worthwhile. Jay and Toby noticed a difference in my attitude, and it gave them something to be excited about, too. Instead of telling their friends that they couldn't come over because Grandma was dying, they were telling their friends to come over and see the new puppy.

And come they did. Toby told his friends that Tyrone was named after his favorite NBA star, Tyrone "Muggsy" Bogues, who played for the Charlotte Hornets. So we bought him a purple collar and decorated it with Hornet colors, and made it so. Jay told his friends he was just a "mutt with a perm," and the delight we took in our new family member was absolute.

The change was not lost on the visiting hospice staff, who noticed the difference as well. The nurses and social workers remarked that the climate in the house was palpably cheerful! Tyrone the puppy at the age of three months touched more lives than could possibly be imagined, and helped to send my mother off, not in an anxiety-ridden and tragic environment, but in an atmosphere of peace. My mother died in my arms, Tyrone and Sable still on the bed beside her, little furry escorts into the bright, white light. Healers with fur coats.

Sable died at the age of twenty-one and Tyrone is now nine years old. Many years later, I still wonder at the difference he made in the life of a dying person and the people around her. I learned then, first-hand, that animals are intuitive therapists. I knew someday I would bring this message to others. I needed to share the important news that animals can make a hopeless situation bearable. Fate intervened many years later when I befriended two wonderful dogs who would become the Hospice Hounds.

2

Pet Therapy Partners

Under the fur coat beats
my sister's heart of gold

A FEW YEARS AFTER MY MOTHER DIED, I found myself working in a charming veterinary practice called Village Animal Clinic. The clinic is owned by two doctors who are married to each other in a stunning example of total opposites attracted to one another. Lisa Degen is strikingly pretty with closely cropped blonde hair and sparkling, intelligent eyes. A vegetarian, she has a petite figure that belies her resolute nature. Lisa is a specialist who works with critically complicated cases. Frantic guardians bring their animal companions from all over Florida to see her. She treats animals diagnosed with cancer, diabetes, thyroid disease, and more life-threatening illnesses. She's a serious doctor with a serious mission, to keep a beloved family member alive and comfortable for just a little longer.

Her husband, Mike Berkenblit (or "Dr. B." as everyone calls him) is forty-five, and survives on coffee, radishes, and boiled eggs. He is tall and athletic, with a laid-back attitude that contrasts sharply with his quick temper. He's a kind boss who throws impromptu pizza luncheons or surprise ice cream parties in the middle of a busy workday. He's popular too with local cat-people and dog rescue groups, who always find him a soft touch who can be counted on for free spay or neuter, heartworm treatment, or emergency euthanasia for strays or wounded animals. It's not at all unusual that he would spread this unique charm to dying patients through his own dogs, Woody and Katie.

These two canine "sisters" idle away their days with their mother and father at the clinic. They are exposed to all kinds of beings—from puppies and kittens to grouchy cats and macho pit bulls. They endure the attentions of overly curious children and sniffing hounds, and spend the day visiting with clients and snoozing in an atmosphere buzzing with activity. They are admired by long-time clients, who bring them goodies to show their respect. Sometimes, when they hear a hospitalized patient meowing or crying, they go to them and sniff at their cage, lying on the floor as near as they can get, something that has a remarkably calming effect on an apprehensive animal.

Thus, Woody and Katie's pet therapy program began with actual pets! If a companion animal is taken to the treatment area for an ear cleaning or pedicure, Woody and Katie visit with the client in the exam room, a "loaner dog" until the owner's own pet is returned to him or her. In the short time that I worked at Village, I grew very attached to these remarkable dogs.

Woody is a yellow Labrador with smiling brown eyes and happy spirit. She is small for a Labrador, and wags her tail gleefully, snapping at the air when she's happy. She catches food treats tossed in the air and is always around when food is near. We had a game we frequently played while I worked at the Village.

When I was quietly absorbed in laboratory tests or paperwork, I would look over at her, sleeping tranquilly on the floor. In a deep sleep, Woody didn't open her eyes, yet still acknowledged me by wagging her tail lazily in response—always seeming to know when I was looking in her direction. In order to fool her, I would surreptitiously look at her from different angles and distances when she was fast asleep. She never failed to delight me with a few thumps of her tail—so special is our friendship.

Katie is an Australian Shepherd with a honey-glazed personality. Her sleepy brown eyes are intensely penetrating. Katie's response to a friendly hello is to simply drop to the ground and roll over on her back in a single motion, begging for a belly rub. Since the technicians and receptionists seldom have time to stop what they are doing and accommodate her, she doesn't always get what she wants. I have seen her follow her quarry around, eyes piercing and demanding, as if the target human is just too dense to get the idea.

These "sisters" have the perfect personality for hospital work, with just one flaw. They are both rabid food hounds, and even hospital food is a coveted treat. Sometimes, having veterinarians for parents isn't always so much fun. When parents are always harping about nutrition and healthy weights, they can be such bores!

One day Woody and Katie came to work very late, accompanied by another employee, Tricia. "Where do you take them?" I asked.

"To hospice," she answered. "They're Delta dogs," she said, referring to the Delta Society, an organization that certifies animals for work as pet therapists. "They go visit the sick people at hospice. But I got married last week and this is my last week here so I guess they won't be going anymore."

I thought back to the overwhelming gratitude I had felt for hospice and all the nurses who were there for us when my mother was dying. I had always wanted to give something back to them. The opportunity to do so was staring me in the face. "Well," I ventured. "What does that entail?"

"Not much, really," Tricia said. "The dogs have already been certified by the Delta Society, and you have to attend a one-day orientation at hospice. Then you just go when you can. If you are interested, I know the dogs would appreciate it, they like going there and nobody else has expressed an interest."

I attended the orientation at the first opportunity. As Matt, the volunteer coordinator, called on us, we introduced ourselves and shared with the group why we wanted to volunteer with hospice. While I wasn't the only volunteer who had personal experience with the center, I was the only new volunteer to sign up for pet therapy. Several others in the room said that they had dogs at home and had always wondered what it would be like to do pet therapy. But their dogs, like my Tyrone, were not the right temperament for hospital work.

Animals involved in pet facilitated therapy must be of a sedate and tolerant nature, unfazed by the presence of other animals, noises, or clinging children. The Delta Society helps to determine which candidates are suitable for this very special brand of pet therapy.

Matt explained to the new volunteers that the dog's temperament was important. If an I.V. line were to get tangled around the dog, he must be trusted to stand perfectly still while it gets untangled. And since patients are allowed to have their own animals come visit, therapy dogs must also be trustworthy around other animals. It isn't necessary to have Delta certification to come to hospice, only proof of current vaccination. "If you have a nice dog, the patients love it when they come to visit them," said Matt. "Everyone here, all the nurses and orderlies, and the chaplain, even most of the doctors know Woody and Katie. I am sure they are as sorry to see Tricia go as I am," he added. I could see why. Tricia was a pretty, young aerobics instructor who positively radiated vitality. As a middle-aged aerobics-*avoider*, I had a tough act to follow. But I loved Woody and Katie and knew that it was they who were the real therapists. I was nothing more than an escort for them. I was very fortunate to have found them; they were just the perfect partners.

3

The Man Who Could Not Eat

*There are provisions for the belly
and provisions for the soul*

KATIE IS SOMETIMES SOUND ASLEEP WHEN WE
leave for hospice, so she doesn't always go on our visits,
and Woody and I go alone. This was such a day. It had
been a terrible day at the clinic for Woody. A grateful client had
gifted the staff with a delicious array of warm bagels, croissants,
and fresh donuts bringing the scent of a warm bakery upon the
clinic. Despite all Woody's efforts to charm her way into the
employees' kitchen for a handout, she was unable to get even one
employee to risk the wrath of her dad (the vet) and give her a
morsel of food. So it was with great enthusiasm that Woody
accepted her invitation to go to hospice and visit the patients.

With tail wagging and pulling uncharacteristically at the lead,
Woody bolted to the car. She knew that someone in hospice
would take pity on her and see her for the starving ragamuffin that
she was. Trevor was always good for a cookie or two. Trevor was
the telephone operator at the center. He loved dogs. Every time
we came to the center, there was Trevor sitting in his cubby-with-
a-window just inside the front door. His face would light up and he
would remind me of his love for dogs. "I love dogs," he would say

happily. "You bring Woody and Katie right over here to Trevor," he would beckon. And they would trot on over and put their paws on the window ledge, standing on their hind legs, and give Trevor sloppy kisses. Trevor would smile his big broad smile and tell Woody and Katie what a beautiful dogs they were. He would take Woody's pale buttery ears in his plump black hands and tell her that she could come visit him anytime.

Sometimes, when we were finished with our visits, I would bring Woody and Katie to stay with Trevor in his cubby-with-a-window so that I could go into the tiny cafeteria and get us a little lunch. Volunteers were treated to lunch. Thanks to the health departments' rule about no dogs in food-service areas, however, we couldn't take advantage of this particular benefit unless Trevor was at work. Lunch usually consisted of a meat sandwich that a vegetarian like myself wouldn't be all that interested in anyway. But I hadn't converted Woody and Katie to vegetarianism yet, so they were always interested. They were, after all, volunteers with official photo-ID hospice badges, so by rights, they too were entitled to nice volunteers' lunches. But on that day, when Woody trotted over to Trevor's cubby-with-a-window, she was greeted with the unsmiling face of a severe woman with pink hair. I could almost hear Woody mutter as she backed away in horror, "Yowzers!" I decided to distract Woody from yet another food issue (she has so many issues that revolve around food). So, with a polite nod to "Pink Hair," we started down the corridor to spread whatever doggie delight we could still muster.

The name on the door of room 101 was "Harry." I never know the patient's last name and this causes me some distress. Having grown up following a generation of people who demanded that young people call them by their title and surnames, I am always uncomfortable with uninvited familiarity. Calling senior strangers by their first name is something that still evokes my mother's voice taking me to task for "taking liberties with someone's name."

We entered the darkened room quietly so as not to disturb the heart-to-heart conversation that surely must have been taking place during this sorrowful period. "Hi," I said somewhat apologetically, "Is this a good time?"

Paula, Harry's daughter, assured me that it was and invited us in. I introduced myself and Woody, explaining that Woody was a therapy dog who came to hospice to visit with the patients. "Oh, well, let's see," Paula said, without much conviction. "Dad, there's a dog here. See the dog, Dad?" I got the sense that Paula may not have been much of a "dog person," but was happy for the distraction.

Harry was straight and tall, sitting up in his bed and quite alert. Since so many of the patients are unable to talk, let alone sit up, Harry seemed comparatively lucid. He appeared to be a tall man, about seventy years of age. I could see his emaciated form beneath the starched white sheets and thin green blankets. His face was drawn and gaunt, his head covered by only a few islands of gray strands of hair. His large, bony hands were covered with transparent, gray skin, lined with ropelike deep blue veins and covered with purple splotches. There was a puffy bruise where an IV needle had once been.

His visitor, a tall middle-aged woman was standing close by, and they were engaged in quiet conversation. She was holding a pink can that contained a nutritional drink with a straw in the opening. On the wheeled tray before Harry was a complete lunch. There was a small bowl of green beans, a plate of mashed potatoes and a small portion of meat loaf, a paper cup of grapes, and a little steaming teapot. The meal was untouched, and, knowing Woody was particularly obsessed with food that day, this caused me slight trepidation.

I urged Woody forward to the head of the bed where she placed her chin by Harry's hand. In a reflex, Harry immediately lifted his hand and pulled away. He and Woody regarded one another for a few moments and I sensed that I was not among animal people. I was about to say goodbye when Harry spoke.

"What does she eat?" he said. His voice was thin, barely above a whisper. It was as though speaking somehow caused him discomfort. But I was happy to have a topic to discuss, any topic. Visiting people who have never enjoyed a kinship with an animal is sometimes awkward, whereas those who have had animals in their lives react to the presence of a dog with warm acceptance. Without that common bond between us, it is a challenge finding ways to make light conversation in the private bedroom of a person you don't know—a person wearing pajamas, a person who is dying.

"Oh, well, eating is Woody's favorite thing to do," I told him brightly. "She's a food hound, loves to eat. Her mom and dad are vets who keep her on a very strict diet of healthy stuff. She hangs out at the clinic with us, and sometimes the employees slip her goodies." Woody looked at me with a "who-are-you-trying-to-kid" look, which I ignored.

"But," Harry persisted. "Can she eat?"

"Yes, of course, she can eat, she loves to eat." I was beginning to suspect I was dealing with medication-induced dementia.

Again, Harry persisted. "Can she eat OK?" he asked with genuine concern. "Is she able to eat whatever she wants?" Harry's face was burdened with anxiety, and I shot a curious look at Paula. She explained that Harry could not eat, for his throat was filled with candida, and he was unable to swallow.

Sometimes, when people become gravely ill, their immune system is weakened. Candida can affect any mucous membrane in the body, and oral candidiasis is common. The presence of such an infection makes it very difficult, even painful, for those patients to swallow, let alone eat. But, incredibly, Harry wasn't thinking of his own discomfort. It dawned on me that he was concerned that Woody may be suffering the same fate and I felt immediate shame for my earlier judgment that he was out of touch or that he didn't care much for animals. It appeared he was very much in touch. I couldn't help but think how this man recognized in another species the ability to experience the same fears that he did. He felt such a kinship with Woody that he projected his own misery upon her.

"Dad," Paula interjected, more softly now. "Woody can eat just fine, Dad, you don't have to worry about her at all, she's fine." Harry never took his eyes off Woody's sweet benevolent face, upturned to look intently in his eyes, too.

"What could they do for her?" he worried aloud. "If she couldn't eat, what could they do?" He reverently placed a wizened hand on Woody's pale yellow head and stroked her gently for a while before closing his eyes.

The four of us stayed in quiet communion for a time. This dying man's concern for an animal he had just met illustrated the interconnectedness among all of us. Woody felt it too, I'm sure of it. For the first time since I've known her, she didn't make a scene begging for food, even though there was a tray laden with food just beyond nose's reach. Especially on this day, I would have expected her to abandon all dignity in a disgraceful show of desperation for a handout. I believe, however, that she sensed Harry's distress, and knew that her own welfare was somehow at the core of his concern. She never took her eyes off him, and I knew that she was communicating all the positive energy she could so as to assuage his fears.

"It's funny," Paula whispered after a time. "He's been asking everyone—the nurses, the social workers, the orderlies—just everyone if they can eat all right. I never considered him much of an animal person. Yet, here he is not even making the distinction that Woody is a dog and not a person, and he's worried if she can eat. I really wonder what that's all about."

I have to say, I wonder too. Not once did he ever ask me if I could eat all right. I was so very proud of Woody and her unselfish display of discipline that I requested of her a "sit, stay" outside the door of the little cafeteria while I slipped inside to procure some peanut butter cookies. She wolfed them down in two bites. With that, Woody the angel dog morphed into Woody the cookie monster and we went about our day.

4

Sato Therapy

Somewhere a hero walks
the street unrecognized

WHEN VOLUNTEERS COME TO THE HOSPICE center for their visit, they sign in and take a briefing list. The handwritten list provides volunteers with helpful information about each patient's situation. The information includes such notations as "Room 101, visit patient and family" indicating that it's all right to stop in even if there is family present; or "Room 102, Patient not conscious, but can hear," meaning that volunteers may sit by the bed and read a book or say a prayer aloud. The notation on Maria's list read "Room 110, Spanish-speaking patient." Not able to speak Spanish, I figured that Katie and Woody's Spanish was about as good as mine, so I took a chance.

A young woman was standing at the foot of Maria's bed, anxiously watching the patient whose breathing was halting and noisy. The inspirations came in sporadic gasps, the expirations followed irregularly, if at all. The doctors call this Cheyne-Stokes breathing, and it can mean death is imminent. The young woman was about thirty and had jet-black hair, tightly curled and cut close to her head. I couldn't see her eyes, as she was looking at the patient. She had wads of tissue in one hand, which wiped her eyes, while she leaned on the foot rail of the bed with the other, as if for support. She was a heavyset woman, wearing a black shapeless dress and flat shoes. Her olive skin was pale, not the characteristic glow of Latino women who seem only to need a drop of sunlight for a radiant bronze. Standing hunched over like she was, shoulders rounded, I got the sense that she was bearing the weight of the world on them.

The aura in the room was heavy and tragic. I felt so sorry for this woman, because she looked like a younger rendering of the woman in the bed, and I knew in an instant this was Maria's daughter. Maria was of similar coloring and hairstyle, but her skin was ashen instead of pale, her hair a silver-blue, and her face contorted. Her black eyes were turned upward, her mouth wide open as she struggled for breath. She was already gone from this world. She was already on her journey. I wasn't sure if I should interrupt what may have been this young woman's very last moments with her mother. I stood in the door for a moment nervously looking for a clue as to what I should do. To my horror, Katie forged ahead and nudged the woman's leg. The visitor's reaction was to look slowly down at Katie, uncomprehending, and then burst into tears. I quickly stepped forward and put my arm around her trembling shoulders, gently leading her to the loveseat. Her body shuddered under the weight of her grief, tears saturating the tissue, shoulders heaving with every racking sob. She was clearly feeling the debilitating impact of what was about to happen.

We sat on the loveseat, my arm around her, while Katie and Woody lay down at our feet. As I sat there, I looked around at the objects in the room. The rooms all have a small bulletin board next to the bed where cards and pictures can be placed at the patient's eye level. A pink crystal rosary was pinned and spread out on the bulletin board, along with a row of neatly arranged mass cards. Small pictures of St. Thérèse of Lisieux and the Blessed Mother were also tacked to the bulletin board. There were several family snapshots of smiling people enjoying family times. On the table was a framed photo of the Sacred Heart of Jesus, and a small bottle with a handwritten label "agua bendita—holy water." The Bible, in Spanish, lay on the bed by the patient's chest, a black rosary on top of it. I reached into my pocket for my mother's rosary, and held the beads in my hand without removing them from my pocket.

After a while the woman seemed spent and composed herself. Then she looked up at me with eyes swollen and red. "Are you a volunteer?" she asked me.

"Yes," I answered. "We all are volunteers." I looked down at Katie and Woody. She also looked at the dogs lying contentedly on the floor and said nothing. "Is this your mom?" I asked, indicating the patient.

"Yes, that's Mom. But I think she's dying today," she said sadly. She told me her name—like her mother's it was Maria. I brought out the rosary I had been concealing in my pocket. I knew that saying the rosary is a powerful meditation and a source of great comfort for some people. The repetition of words serve to quiet

the mind and the spirit much like a mantra. I knew this from
many years before when I shared the rosary with my mother, and
my critically ill mother-in-law before her. So I asked Maria if she
would like to say it together. She nodded yes without saying a
word. She didn't move toward the rosary on the bed, but simply
sat there and continued to look at Katie and Woody. She seemed
confused about their presence. "They let you bring dogs in here?"
she asked. "I never heard of a hospital where they let dogs come
in. How come they don't make you leave them outside?"

" Well," I began. "Hospices are dedicated to making sure that
their patients are comfortable and their needs are met. Some
people need to be around animals. It's called pet therapy."

"They *need* animals?" she said, still not understanding. "Why
on earth would someone need animals?" She was looking at me as
if she was missing something. The look on her face was pure
innocence, and I knew that she was not annoyed at the presence
of two large dogs, but fascinated. "We don't really like dogs too
much where I come from," she explained. "We never had a dog or
anything. And in Catano, where I live in Puerto Rico, I see the
dogs on the street. They don't look anything like these dogs
though. We call them *satos*; they're just street dogs that nobody
cares about. They die in the streets. They won't let them in
hospitals that's for sure."

"How sad for the people that they don't understand how
wonderful dogs can be," I said. Maria never took her eyes off
Woody and Katie, who were taking the opportunity to enjoy a nap
on the cool tile floor. So we sat in silence. Maria had been crying

when we came in the room, but her mind was back in Catano now, thinking of the *satos* on the street. Finally, Maria asked if she should be petting them. Katie had rolled over on her back and was exposing her tummy, ever ready for a belly rub.

"Sure," I told her. "That's why they're here." Maria tentatively put out her hand and patted Katie on her soft belly. Katie groaned in pleasure and Maria pulled her hand away, alarmed. "She growls?" she asked me. "Why did she growl? Doesn't she like that?" I smiled and told her that Katie was simply giving a sigh of relief that someone had finally noticed that she had assumed the belly-rub position. "You seem to have a way with dogs, Maria," I said. Maria looked down at Katie and told her how pretty she was.

Katie has no tail, being an Aussie. But when she is happy she moves the two sacral vertebrae to which a tail would be attached if there was one. This makes for a barely perceptible movement and lends some mystery to her emotions. But Woody wagged her big yellow tail enough for both of them.

Maria reached down and stroked Katie again, very gingerly, and didn't say anything more. I sat on the floor beside Woody and rubbed her ears and head. I stayed very quiet, willing this spiritual union to continue so Maria could enjoy the brief break from her grief. After a while Maria looked over at her mother. "She looks so peaceful, really," she said. "Her breathing….But still, she isn't hurting and it's like she's sleeping with her eyes open. I wonder why I was so scared before?" I told her that this is why dogs come to hospice, to take away the fear; and that Woody and Katie's mere presence is calming.

Maria was amazed. "I had never realized what consolation a dog could bring and I never thought that an animal could bring such a sense of peace and comfort," she said. She got up off the loveseat and went to her mother's bedside. She stood there for a moment, looking down at her, and then gently lifted the rosary from the Bible. She came back over to us, and joined us on the floor. She sat next to Katie and I stayed by Woody. And with both of us keeping one hand on a sleeping dog, while holding a rosary in the other, together we quietly recited the rosary.

After we said the last of the "Our Fathers," we sat in silence for a moment longer. Then I got to my feet, and the dogs did so as well. I told Maria that I might not see her again, but I would keep her and her mother in my prayers. "Can I call you in a few weeks?" she asked.

"Sure," I said, reaching for a business card to give her.

"That's good, thank you," she said. "Because I was thinking maybe you can teach me how I can do dog therapy, too."

My heart filled with joy at this idea. I hope that, someday, a starving dog somewhere will be plucked off a street corner in Puerto Rico, cleaned up, sent to school, and become a fine pet therapist.

5

A Deathbed Confession

Will God forgive me
for what I have done?

I T WAS IN THE MIDDLE OF THE FUROR AFTER THE
2000 presidential election and Leroy was in the final stages of
AIDS. His eyes were big and round, his lips cracked and
parched, his teeth showing white in a grotesque, skeletal grin. He
had open and oozing sores about his face and neck and all over his
arms. The sores were covered with bandages in a vain attempt to
contain the blood, but the bandages were soaked and needed to be
changed on the hour. He was emaciated. His bony arms and legs
were spindly and as fragile as a single dainty finger of a small
porcelain statue. His once black skin was now ashen and gray, and
his head was covered not with hair, but scabs. He was dying that
day.

Woody and Katie and I entered Leroy's room and were
immediately assaulted by most unpleasant smells: urine, blood,
and something unidentifiable. I was almost hoping Leroy was
asleep so I wouldn't have to stay, but he was wide-awake and quite
chatty. The television set was tuned to CNN and blaring out from
the wall. "Hello, sir," I said as I entered the room. "I wonder if you

like dogs at all." Leroy immediately hit the mute button on his remote, and turned his attentions fully to me.

"Come in, come in, I was just laying here wondering if we'll have a president before I die! My brother told me he even met the Rev. Jesse Jackson himself last week! Man, I wish I could have been there too. My name is Leroy, and what is yours?" he asked. His manner was unmistakably warm and hospitable.

"My name is Michelle, and my partners are Woody and Katie." I introduced them one at a time.

"Well, hello Woody, and what kind of a dog are you?" he looked directly at her. Woody simply wagged her tail and offered a happy canine grin, so I answered for her. "She's a yellow Lab, Leroy." He asked how old she was, why she seemed so small for a Lab, and if maybe she should be bred to a larger dog, so as to make her puppies larger.

"Oh, no!" I said. "They're a little too old now for that, and they have been spayed for a very long time now." Leroy nodded that he understood. He then said hello to Katie, and asked about her age as well.

"A Shepherd you say? I don't think I know about these Shepherds. I have heard of German Shepherds, but this is Australian? Is that where they come from?" he asked. Despite the look and smell of death in the room Leroy was effortlessly making conversation with me. I have come to the conclusion that no matter what happens within the hospice setting, everything passes for normal.

I explained that Katie was an Australian Shepherd and that, like German Shepherds, she was a member of the herding group. "They commonly refer to them as Aussies," I said. "They originally came from Australia, but they really got their start in California. They are not quite as popular for companions yet, but it's coming to that. They have the same temperament as a Labrador or a Golden, a little more gentle and friendly than the German Shepherd dog. They are smaller too, only getting to be about fifty pounds, where the German Shepherd dog is much bigger than that. *She's* a tri-color, but they come in lots of different colors, whereas the German Shepherd only comes in black and tan, and maybe white, though some people don't believe the white ones are true German Shepherds."

Leroy was listening politely to my lesson in breed identification. He seemed sincerely interested. Despite the foul odor in the room, I was beginning to feel comfortable with him and wanted to visit a little longer. He appeared to appreciate the break from watching the endless political news on television. This was, after all, Palm Beach County, home of the infamous butterfly ballot that proved so confusing to voters, and there wasn't much else on TV. He was certainly enjoying the attentions of Woody and Katie, who had been alternatively licking his hands and investigating a crumpled-up donut bag on the floor under Leroy's bed. Woody had been snapping the air and nudging his hand, when she accidentally hit the nurse's call button. A nurse immediately appeared at the door. "Hi Leroy, what can I do for you?" she said pleasantly. "Well now Woody, you done called the

nurse out!" Leroy said to Woody, "Tell the lady what you need."
And we laughed at the little mishap. The nurse told Woody how
beautiful she was and that she could call on her any time, and she
left us alone again.

"I have a dog too," said Leroy.

I was pleased to hear this news, and eager to hear about
Leroy's dog. "What kind of dog do you have?" I asked him.

"He's a pit bull. Big dog. Red nose pit," he said.

I made a face and told him that I loved pit bulls because they
are so handsome and strong, but I really hated that some people
use them for fighting.

"Oh, I did too," said Leroy. "He was the best damn fighter in
town!"

I was troubled by this information, of course, but wanted to
hear what he had to say, so I went along with him.

"Well, Leroy, didn't that make you feel bad? I mean, weren't
you afraid your dog would get hurt? I guess what I am saying is, just
look at Woody and Katie here, you wouldn't want anyone to hurt
them or make them fight for their lives, would you?" I asked.

"Yeah, I know." Leroy said. "I decided a while back I was
gonna just leave it alone. I saw my friend's dog; he had scars all
over him. And, once, this guy I know, he took a stick and knocked
out all his dog's teeth because he was so mad at him for losing a
fight. Then he took that dog down to Miami and he had all these
metal teeth put in. Brought him back to the neighborhood and
was just bragging to everyone about his dog and his new fangs.
Spent $7,000 on that dog's teeth! Then that night, someone stole

the dog right out from his cage. They never found that dog. And sometimes, some people kill their dogs right on the spot for losing. The first time I saw that, it made me feel that this is wrong, you know? I knew it was illegal, but damn if I didn't know it was also sinful what we was doing to them dogs, they being God's creatures and all."

I nodded in agreement, and looked down at Woody and Katie, telling them again how nobody would ever hurt them. "These guys are my best friends," I said. "I can't imagine letting anyone hurt them. I would rather die than let anything happen to my friends here, they are so sweet I just can't imagine that."

"Well, you know, they all God's creatures and I guess it was a bad thing what we did," Leroy said after a while. "I've been trying to get right with God ever since I found out just how sick I really was. I've been trying to do good. It's been a long time since I made that dog fight. I don't let nobody fight Chester no more."

I asked Leroy if Chester was still alive, and where he was now. "My brother has him. He keeps him in the house with him. He's a great watchdog. He'll be out in the yard, and someone will come along, and they will be walking along the fence, and Chester just follows them along the fence, not making a sound, not a word out of him, and he will just watch the man walk along the fence, and then he watches until he isn't near our property anymore. He never makes a sound."

"I remember reading somewhere that silence is the mark of a talented watchdog," I responded. They keep very still, very quiet, and then pounce if someone does something they find threatening. "I think your Chester makes a much better friend and protector than he does a fighter, huh?"

"You got that right," he said. "These dogs good watchdogs?" he asked, indicating Woody and Katie.

"I don't really know about that." I said, "I don't live with them. But I know they have a lot of other talents, like visiting people in hospice. So they do their part in this world: I think that's what's important."

"Seeing these dogs, I feel kind of bad for what I put Chester through," Leroy said. "I think these kids are all doing it. They think it's a big deal, makes them feel like a big man, you know what I'm saying? You think God's gonna forgive me for what I did to Chester?" Leroy was intensely studying his fingers and not looking at me. I didn't know what to say. I find it hard to forgive animal cruelty no matter how it rears its ugly head, but I was fairly certain that God was a lot more tolerant than I am. And I knew Woody and Katie certainly were. They never stopped competing for Leroy's attentions, not even when they heard what crimes he had committed against their own kind. I didn't answer right away, though I knew in my heart what Leroy was longing to hear.

"I think maybe you should call your brother and ask him to bring Chester around to see you," I said. "Maybe give him a kiss on his precious red nose; tell him he's special. I think maybe that's what you need. I think you need for your brother to see you do that, so he knows to keep Chester out of harm's way. That's what I think you should do."

"You know, maybe I will," Leroy agreed. "I think that's a good idea. I think maybe I will do just that very thing."

Just then, the music therapist came in with his guitar and asked Leroy if he would like to hear a song or two. "I'm Leroy, sir," he said. "What's your name?" Still being polite and cordial, Leroy learned the music man's name was Gregory and that he was there to take musical requests of any kind. "Well, Gregory, I do appreciate your stopping by, I surely do. But you know, I think I have a phone call to make right about now and I don't have much time. But you see I have a Bible right here by my bed, so maybe you can come back a little later and we can sing some Bible songs. How about that?"

Gregory agreed to come back later and, with a nod to the dogs and me, he said goodbye. Leroy reached out his hand to shake hands with me, and I approached his bed so I could reach him. He held my hand for a moment and thanked me for stopping by to visit.

"You are so welcome, sir," I told him. "I hope I get to meet your Chester next time I come in. I hope your brother brings him in soon." In my heart I hoped it would be soon enough for Leroy.

"I'm going to call him right now and ask him to do that," Leroy said. "And then I'm going to have me a little talk with my Creator. Chester's and my Creator that is, ain't that right?"

"It is," I told him.

It is so right.

6

Preacher, Step Aside

*To be together again in eternity,
I will meet you on the other side*

J OSEPH'S SUN-BRIGHTENED ROOM WAS OCCUPIED
by a small crowd of people. But despite this jovial setting, the
feeling in the room was gray. Five people were standing quietly
around the bed, and a minister was standing over the patient, his
back to the door. He was reading quite loudly from a Bible. Woody
and I were working alone that day, Katie had not wanted to yield
her snoozing spot to the other clinic dog, a Chihuahua-mix named
Darby who accompanied her mom, Dr. Prior, who also works at
the clinic.

We waited silently just outside the door, unobserved for a
moment so as not to interrupt what may have been Joseph's last
rites. The reading sounded somewhat perfunctory, as if the reader
was speaking not so much *to* his listeners, as *at* them. The reader
was finishing the Twenty-Third Psalm—"Only goodness and
kindness follow me all the days of my life; and I shall dwell in the
house of the Lord for years to come…"—so I quietly took a few
steps into the room. The preacher flipped his pages in preparation
for the next reading, and the patient stared uninterestedly at the
television set mounted on the wall with muted sound. Among the

visitors were a very tall, brown-haired boy who looked to be about fifteen years old and his mother, also tall, also brunette. They were, I was to later learn, Joseph's sister and nephew. The other woman in the room was Joseph's wife, Sherry, a sad, pretty woman with strawberry blonde hair. She, too, was tall and dressed in jeans and a bright red sweater. Sherry was being embraced by a man who looked to be in his sixties—Joseph's dad.

There was also a small, tow-headed child, about six, sitting in the big armchair. This beautiful child was Joseph's little boy. It was he who saw us first, and drew in a breath. The visitors facing the door followed the child's gaze and noticed us, reacting with surprise and delight. The pastor stopped reading and looked up at them, then at us. As it registered why we were there, a hint of rejection crossed his face.

The preacher turned to the patient and, with a tone usually employed by one addressing the hard of hearing, asked "You're not a dog lover, are you Joseph?" To which Joseph answered with a most assertive "*Yes!*" That's all Woody and I needed to hear and we took this response as an invitation to enter. I swiftly maneuvered Woody past the reverend, who was not surrendering his place easily, and brought her bedside.

"What's her name?" Joseph asked.

"This is Woody. She's my partner." I introduced myself as well. "I know she has a boy's name but she's a girl. She loves to come here."

"Well hi, girl," Joseph said, and stroked Woody on the head for a moment. The others in the room asked a lot of questions about Woody—how old she was, whom she lived with, and how the pet therapy program works. We talked about Woody, who was suddenly the center of all the attention (her preferred situation by far). I fielded all the questions while Joseph continued to pat Woody on the head and pet her, speaking to her like an old school pal.

The teenager spoke up. "Uncle Joe," he said. "Remember Gordon? She looks like Gordon; only Gordon was a little more brown, remember Uncle Joe?"

"I do," answered Joseph weakly. Joseph was a young man, about forty-two. And although he had a muscular build, disease had made him appear aged and decrepit. "I surely do." Still looking at Woody, he launched into the story of Gordon, a Labrador mix who had come to him on a miserably hot Georgia day. Joseph was just twenty-five at the time, and serving in the Army. "I was stationed in Georgia," he remembered. "And I was grilling some burgers, just drinking a few beers with my wife and my friend Carlos. We'd both just got promotions to staff sergeant, and we were celebrating that we would be heading over to the European theater in a few months. All of a sudden we saw these two dogs just trotting down the side of the highway. It was a busy road that we lived on and I was scared they were gonna get hit by a car or something. It was so hot out I swear there was steam coming off the asphalt on the road. Man, I am telling you, their tongues were hanging out! So I called to them. They came running over like I was a long lost friend. I mean, they didn't hesitate for a second. As soon as they saw me waving them over, they just came running over like it was me they were looking for! It was great!" Joseph smiled at the memory.

I shot a furtive look at the preacher, who was standing stiffly at the foot of the bed, feigning interest. As the tale of Gordon's rescue unfolded, a remarkable thing happened. Joseph's voice became clear, full of vitality and enthusiasm. He appeared to be getting younger before our eyes. The others in the room noticed it as well. They exchanged delighted little smiles. Joseph continued his story. "I gave the dogs water and some burgers and other stuff around the house, and Sherry gave them a bath. They were so hot and dirty, and, oh my God, they were covered with fleas, remember honey?" He looked over at his pretty wife, her face devoid of makeup and swollen from sleepless grief-filled nights. She was still leaning against her father-in-law. His arm was around her and her head was resting on his capable chest. His face, too, had softened with the tale, and I was suddenly aware of a tragic and strange reality. The young man lying in the hospital bed actually appeared older than his own father. Joseph's young features were clouded by the specter of a fatal disease and made him look unnaturally aged. Sherry had been listening to her husband with a look of warm remembrance, and nodded enthusiastically at Joseph's question. She couldn't trust herself, I'm sure, to utter a single word for fear of ruining the happy moment with an emotional release of tears. Joseph hadn't noticed; he was lost in a fog of remembrance.

Joseph's little son was standing by the bed, petting Woody lovingly, kissing her head, and listening with rapt attention to the story his father was telling. He was captivated by Woody, the story, and the transformation in his Dad. Woody was every bit the picture of angelic joy. "We let 'em hang around for a few days," Joseph continued. "We kept the Lab and called him Gordon. And we gave the Rottie mix to my friend Paul. Man, we had Gordon for ten years. He was the best dog I ever had. I never got another one. How could I? He was the best." His voice trailed off and he was looking at Woody, remembering his old friend. "Wow, I hadn't thought of Gordon in years," he whispered. For a few moments we stood in silence, thinking of two old friends trotting down a dangerous highway and being invited to dinner and life anew. The reverend cleared his throat, but nobody looked his way.

Finally, Sherry spoke up carefully. She looked intently into my eyes. "Joey was very attached to Gordon, you know?" she said. "The Army even flew that dog to Ramstein when we got sent over there, and then back again when our time was up. They were always together. I mean, they went everywhere together. He took him to the beach, out on his boat, on fishing trips, just everywhere. So, I told Joey about the Rainbow Bridge, you know about that, right?" I nodded that I did. "I told him that Gordon is probably at the Rainbow Bridge, waiting for all of us. I mean, don't you think we'll see our pets again when we get to heaven?" Her question was more suited perhaps for the preacher to answer, but Sherry wasn't asking him. I read the message in the look she gave me.

The others in the room looked at me expectantly, but it was the preacher who spoke up. "Doggie Heaven?" he said, laughing like he had made a joke. My eyes met hers but I responded to the preachers' remark.

"No," I said firmly, "*Heaven.*"

"Of course there are no animals in Heaven," he replied coldly. He scanned the room for an ally, but there was none. This was a group of animal-lovers and he was completely outnumbered.

"Really?" I asked. "Not according to Revelation. You're the Bible expert," I said respectfully. "But I know that in Revelation we read that white horses will be coming from Heaven."

"Oh, *them?*" he replied dismissively. "No, I'm sorry, but they're bad animals. They are not exactly pets."

"Oh, I see," I said smiling at the group. "Bad animals, right. Well, the riders may have been bad, I have to agree with you there, with all those bows and swords and stuff. But I can assure you there are no bad animals. All animals are good. They're God's creatures aren't they?" I looked at the group and explained that my mother had been a Bible teacher who taught me about the horses coming from Heaven. I told them that when she died, she knew she would see Patrick, the Irish Water Spaniel we brought with us when we moved to Florida from New York. Of this she had no doubt, and she knew the Bible like nobody's business. I shared with them my belief that my Siamese cat Sable was up there too. I was sure of it; she was waiting for me to come and be with her again. "I just hope it's very sunshiny up there," I told them. "Sable loved to snooze in the sun."

The little group nodded and smiled agreeably. They had loved and lost pets in their lives too, and they were certain they would see them in Heaven. It was settled, and Sherry's question had been sincerely answered. Joseph would see his beloved Gordon again. He knew that, of course. But the reassurance of a matter of faith conveyed to someone about to make a journey into the unknown is of such importance that it bears repeating. Woody's presence in that room at that moment guided Joseph and his anxious family on a joyous stroll down a path to a happier era in their lives. She brought them back to a time when a young soldier and his wife had a future full of promise and prosperity. Woody was the catalyst for Joseph's indulging in a fond memory of days past. But she was also instrumental in him bringing the assurance his troubled mind needed; a promise of a heaven where we will once again be united with our loved ones of all species.

And Woody's presence evoked even more. She was Gordon's escort, and Gordon was never far from Joseph's heart anyway. She brought Gordon back in spirit so as to leave him with Joseph, to be his companion once again in the hours when nobody is visiting and Joseph is alone with his frightening thoughts. Gordon helped his master begin his afterlife anew as Joseph had done for a troubled and homeless dog some twenty years ago. Gordon was with us in the room, and we all felt that. It was a moment that was there and then gone.

Woody's gift to Joseph and his family that day was beyond anything that a preacher or a nurse or a doctor could offer. Woody's gift to Joseph was hope—a precious offering at a time when all expectations, anticipation, and optimism are declared medically impossible. Woody didn't know that to give a hopeless person the promise of something better is so priceless a gift that it is beyond our mortal comprehension. She was just doing what she does best, touching a life on the way to another dimension. It took the dog lovers in the room to recognize what had taken place. Indeed, I almost felt sorry for the preacher and the limits to which he was bound. How sad for him that he couldn't see the miracle that had taken place before our very eyes; the restoration of hope to a hopeless man! In truth, love knows no limits. It is forever crossing boundaries of color, age, gender, religion, geography, and, yes, species. Indeed, it just wouldn't be Heaven without those we love. All of them.

7

Denial

*The trustworthy hound
is a girl's best friend*

I T WAS A GRAY, RAINY DAY AS WOODY, KATIE, AND
I quickly made our way through the puddles in the parking lot
to the door of the center. We peeked in room after room, but
the patients all seemed to be dozing, and there weren't many
visitors either. The few visitors who had braved the weather were
themselves napping in the rooms on chairs and on loveseats, soap
operas droning on to uninterested audiences. The rooms, usually
so merry and full of Florida sunshine, were depressingly dingy and
cheerless on this day as the dark clouds threw shadows into the
patient rooms. I decided to wait a few minutes and perhaps try
again in little while. I didn't really want to run back out to the car
in the rain anyway, as much as I loved the smell of wet fur coats
and the challenge of muddy paws.

I brought Woody and Katie over to Trevor, and we chatted a
little about how sad hospice seemed on a day like today, as though
even the skies are sad for the people who are dying here in our
corner of the world. Trevor offered to watch "the girls" while I
slipped into the cafeteria to see what snacks I could find for them.
When I returned, I placed some bowls of water near the fountain

in the atrium and went back to Trevor's cubby-with-a-window for Woody and Katie. I handed Trevor a small plate of oatmeal and chocolate chip cookies. With a wink I said, "Trevor, I always told my sons when they were little that there was not a single thing that could be wrong that chocolate couldn't fix, so I brought you some!" He smiled broadly and laughed out loud. Then he thanked me for the treat, and I left with the dogs to share some cookies with them in the atrium.

Despite the gloom that held the rest of the center in its grip, the atrium was cheery and bright, with strong lights and bright green trees. It was a nice place to take a little break from the sadness that was so much a part of a place where people's souls depart their bodies and loved ones say goodbye. The three of us sat on the floor by the fountain sharing cookies, rolls, and crackers. I was absentmindedly petting the dogs, lost in my thoughts, when a woman and her teenage daughter passed us by. The mother turned back around to look us.

"Are you doing pet therapy?" she asked.

I told her I was.

"Did you go into room 125?" she asked.

I consulted my list to be sure the room was included, then answered that I had gone into that room, but that the patient was fast asleep. "Do you think you could try again?" the woman continued. "It's my mother. We are just going in to see her and I am sure she would love to see the dogs. Her name is Nancy; I'm Helen. Please look for us, OK?" I promised I would.

With all of the cookies and crackers gone, we were ready to try the rounds again and we found a few of the patients were now awake and happy to see us. About an hour later, I found room 125 where Helen and her daughter were waiting for us, and we entered the room.

The room was darker than most because the shades were drawn tight. In the bed lay an elderly woman very close to death. She was staring up at the ceiling, her mouth wide open, one hand by her cheek, the other by her side. Her mouth was covered with white ulcers, and her green eyes were clouded and dull. The sound of her breathing, so strained and shallow, the frozen look on her face, with eyes open and unblinking, were all indications that death was imminent. She was not aware, suspended as she was somewhere between here and the hereafter. Helen's daughter stood just inside the door, head down, not acknowledging our presence. I stood for a moment at the foot of the bed, taking in this unfortunate scene, not knowing what to do or say. Katie and Woody sat quietly on either side of me, quietly waiting for a cue.

"Look Mom," Helen said brightly, "Look, you know how you love dogs." The patient didn't respond. "C'mon Mom," she said again. "This will make you happy. I made sure they came to see you special."

"What are their names?" Helen had a strained, impatient tone in her voice, and after I answered her, she persisted. "Bring them closer. Bring them where she can see them. She can't see them way over there." I drew closer to the bed and lifted Woody by her front paws so she was standing erect, her head even with the patient's face. Still, the patient did not see her.

"Gee, I don't know," Helen apologized. "She really loves dogs. I don't know why she isn't reacting to Woody at all. Maybe she will wake up later; maybe she's just asleep." She leaned in closer and tried again, louder now. "Are you sleeping, Mom? Do you want them to come back later?" Then she looked back at me with an apologetic smile. "Why don't you come back later, OK? I am sure she will be awake in a few minutes and if you could just wait...."

Just then, her daughter interrupted. Still just inside the doorway, she was crying now, looking at her mother in disbelief and anger.

"Mom," said the girl. "Mom, don't be so stupid. She's not going to wake up later." The girl looked at me and rolled her eyes, embarrassed by what she saw has her mom's ignorance.

"Don't you yell at me, Cary!" Helen shot back, her own voice shaking with emotion. "You don't know anything about it, do you? You never want to come here, you are so self-absorbed. I have to drag you to visit your grandmother. What do you know? You don't know anything about it."

Helen was crying now and Cary had flung her backpack to the floor and had dropped down beside it, squatting with her head in her hands, crying too. I was standing between them, and at that moment truly wished I had braved the raindrops and was anywhere but here. Not being a therapist, I didn't know how to handle this emotional outburst, this terribly private moment between a mother and daughter. Katie tugged at her lead, so I unfastened it from her collar. She sauntered over to Cary and dropped to her belly, facing her. Cary looked up, but ignored her. There was a backpack lying next to the teenager, and Katie was sniffing at it intently. Cary pushed her away, but Katie came right back. Helen had taken a seat and was pulling tissues out of a holder when she spoke.

"Five years ago, my mom had a stroke," she said softly.

Cary had reached into her backpack and pulled out a peanut butter sandwich wrapped in cellophane, the object of Katie's intense interest. She opened the wrapping and Woody came bounding over too, tail wagging. As Cary broke off little pieces of the sandwich and fed them to Woody and Katie, she looked up at her mother.

"Mom had a stroke five years ago," Helen repeated. "She couldn't talk. She couldn't talk for over two years. Not saying a word. She was in a nursing home. Cary was only ten so I didn't bring her to the home but once. It was so depressing and I didn't want her to be sad all the time. She and my mom were very close because Mom practically raised her while I was working and going to school. And they used to go to dog shows together, and talk about all the breeds of dogs and share all kinds of little nonsensical trivia about them. It was a game they played. They would query one another endlessly on breed facts, and test each other's knowledge. They always said they were going to get a dog together and travel around to all the shows, just the two of them and the dog, and win lots of ribbons. Mom was even going to find someone to teach Cary to be a professional handler. They never did, because they never could agree on what breed to get. Mom wanted a Saluki, but Cary wanted a dog she could play with, she wanted a Golden or maybe a Lab."

I looked over at Cary who was stroking Woody and Katie softly. I wondered what she was thinking, and if yellow Labradors or Australian Shepherds were ever on her short list of dogs to take to the shows to win ribbons for her and her grandmother.

"One day," Helen continued. "When I was at the nursing home reading to my mother, a girl from the humane society came and she had a puppy with her. It was a big puppy, and she was carrying him around in her arms. She would go from room to room and put the puppy on the patient's beds. When she came in my mom's room, I took the puppy from her and showed her to my mother. My mom was in a wheelchair, so I knelt down and put the puppy on her lap, holding him there. She put her hands on him and she opened her mouth and said: *dog*." Helen looked up at me and smiled a brave smile. "We were blown away! We couldn't believe it. I ran to get the nurse and the nurses came in and we were all crying and laughing because my mom hadn't spoken in two years, and then out of the blue she said *dog*. I don't know. I guess I was hoping for another miracle."

Cary had given the dogs the entire sandwich and was petting them simultaneously, listening to the story. "That's not going to happen again Mom," she said, and looked at me and rolled her eyes again, fearful that I might think her mom uncool for telling me this story and naïve for hoping for a miracle.

I decided it was time to leave mother and daughter alone with their memories. I turned to say goodbye to Helen and told her I would be back again another day. "Maybe she will be more awake another day," I said as I put my hand on her arm, a weak gesture of sympathy and companionship.

"Yes," she agreed. "Come back another day." As we left the room, I told Cary that I would pray for her, and hope to see her competing in a dog show one day. She gave me a small smile and asked me if Woody or Katie had ever been in a dog show. "No," I said. "They're spayed so they can't compete in dog shows. I guess you know all about those rules. But, you know what? I read somewhere that best friends don't need a pedigree to be the best. So I don't think dogs need to go to dog shows to be champions, do you?" I whispered and nodded in Woody and Katie's direction, as if not wanting them to hear.

"You're right," she said, as she walked me to the hallway. "Woody and Katie are better than dog show champions any time." She squatted down to look the dogs in the eye one at a time while kissing their sweet, sweet noses. "You guys are the true champions of the dog world. The real champions."

Woody and Katie responded with generous kisses and enthusiastic tail-wagging. "Will you really come back to see Grandma?" Cary asked. "I don't know," I said. "But maybe if I do you can take Katie's lead and come around the rooms with me, be a real 'handler.' How about that?"

"Cool," said Cary.

Very cool, thought I.

8 ⬱

Squirrel Therapy

Aloha, Shalom, and Woof
—Hello, I love you, and goodbye

AS I APPROACHED THE ROOM I COULD HEAR sounds of laughter. "Oh that stupid bitch!" A woman's voice cried out. This was followed by gales of laughter and agreement. "She hasn't a clue he's cheating on her!" said the voice again. "Well, she deserves what she gets, that's for sure," said another voice, weaker but full of conviction. My curiosity got the best of me and I guess the dogs noticed the gaiety too because their tails began to wag even before we entered the room. People were happy somewhere, and we were going to join in!

The instant I entered the room I knew I would be welcome. On the table by the wall were framed photos of animals in various shapes and sizes and species. The room actually had a congenial, almost festive atmosphere. The occupants of the room were three women: the patient, Dottie, as well as two, much younger women. One young woman was on the couch, the other in the chair. The visitors were excited to see the dogs.

"Look, Aunt Dot," they fussed. "Dogs came to see you. Big wonderful, beautiful dogs! Look at these dogs!" And they collapsed in laughter and silliness. I was so enamored of the photos in the frame that I paid no attention to the women, fixated as I was on the photos. It didn't matter, Woody and Katie were already "working the crowd." The women fussed noisily over them, telling them how beautiful they were, how wonderful it was to see them. It was a girl party, and Woody and Katie were just two more "girls."

The photos that held me in fascination were of animals in silly positions. The first photo was a fat orange cat simply sitting quietly, looking at the camera, but with a perfectly balanced bright green parakeet atop his head. The same cat appeared in the next photo, this time reclining, a fat white rat resting companionably by his side, the cat's tail draped affectionately over the rat's body. The third was of a large hound dog laying on his back with all fours spread apart, long floppy ears spread out on the floor, the dog very much at rest.

I reluctantly turned my attention from the charming photos to Dottie and asked her about the animals in the pictures. She was sitting up in the bed, wearing a silk, hot pink bed jacket. She had a funny yellow hat on her head, the kind they used to wear in the 1970s, knitted and spangled with glittery gold pailettes. Dottie's nieces, MaryAnn and Julie, had been to visit every day of her weeklong "incarceration" as they called it. MaryAnn was seated next to Dottie, giving her a manicure and applying a fiery red polish. Julie was sitting across from them both, providing a running commentary on the soap opera that was playing on the TV. Dottie was very chatty and told me all about her cat Callie that she had had to leave at home. Callie was eighteen years old and the apple of Dottie's eye. She told me all about how Callie spent her days sleeping in the sunshine, grooming herself. She was the cat in the pictures with the bird and the rat.

After a few moments, MaryAnn called out: "Ooh, Ooh, here he is again!" The talk and activity stopped as all attention was turned to the sliding glass door and the patio where a plump squirrel was leisurely selecting a seed from a pile of seeds, nuts, and fruit that had been arranged there. Before long, he was joined by another, and then another, as they made their way to the food and appeared to be carefully choosing the nut or seed of their choice! I was unsure how Katie and Woody would react so I attempted to distract them. Finally, however, the dogs saw the squirrels and, when they did, did nothing more than stand perfectly still, ears and tails erect (well, Woody's tail was erect), bodies stiff, and not making a sound. It was their finest moment of best behavior!

"They come right up to the door, two or three of them at a time and take their sweet time picking out a treat," Julie said. Dottie couldn't take her eyes off them, staring at them with wonder and delight.

"Sometimes," said Dottie. "The squirrels come in the room."

"Oh yes," said the girls together.

Talking all at once they told me that they sometimes left the door open and put the food just inside, just to see what the squirrels would do.

"They actually come right in," said Dottie.

"Yeah," said Julie, shaking her head. "But then Nurse Ratchet comes in and yells at us!"

The four of us laughed at this.

"Yeah, that Nurse Ratchet," said Dottie. "We gotta watch out for that one! Probably doesn't have a boyfriend, probably goes home to a mean old housecat and overdue bills!" At this we all laughed so hard that we frightened the squirrels—who looked up at us in alarm and scurried off. No sooner were they gone but the blue jays took their places, strutting around and grabbing up sunflower seeds and peanuts. We all stared at them in awe, Woody and Katie still not moving even a whisker, sitting perfectly still. I was so proud of them.

We were having such a lovely time that I hated to leave, but it was time to go and so we said goodbye, promising to spread the word about the squirrel food to other patients, but keeping it secret from the nurses who may not be so amused.

When I returned to the clinic, I told Dr. B. about the squirrels and how wonderful Woody and Katie had been, sitting there like angels, never making a sound. "In fact, I don't think I have ever heard Katie bark, not once."

Dr. B. called Katie to him, and she looked at him expectantly. "Katie," he whispered, "Where's the squirrel?" At this, Katie jumped and whirled around the room in an excited frenzy. She was barking in anticipation and searching wildly, nose in the air, while I stood watching in utter disbelief.

Several days later, I returned to the center and went straight to Dottie's room. The room was darkened, and I bumped into the doctor who was just leaving and we nodded hello. A woman who had not been there on my last visit was lying on the loveseat, a blanket over her, talking quietly with Dottie. "Hello," I said. "I was here a few days ago and Dottie enjoyed Woody and Katie...." At the sound of my voice, Dottie looked over at me and motioned for us to come forward.

She was lying in the bed now, the hot pink bed jacket lying on the chair. She was no longer wearing the hat, and she looked very tired. The vertical blinds were drawn across the doors so that the squirrels, if they were there, could not be seen. "Hi sweethearts," Dottie said to the dogs. Her voice was weary and sad. "Come on over here, girls," she beckoned to the dogs.

I let go of the leads and Woody and Katie immediately went to the blinds and nosed an opening so that they could see out. "Oh," whispered Dottie. "They're looking for the squirrels. They're there, I guess. I was bothered by the light, so we closed the curtains." The woman on the loveseat stood up and introduced herself to me, shaking my hand firmly, all professionalism and businesslike. She was aloof, not at all like the casual, funny girls I had met on my earlier visit.

"I'm Dottie's daughter, Ann," she said. Ann was very well dressed in a navy-blue, form-fitting designer suit, and she was tall, with pretty black hair and brown eyes. She looked to me to be an executive. She had kicked off her shoes and was standing in her stocking feet. I introduced myself and Woody and Katie, and explained that we had been in a few days earlier and had met Julie and MaryAnn. "Yes, my cousins," Ann said. "They went back to Michigan."

Ann approached Woody and Katie and gently led them away from the window, cooing to them and praising them for being so good. She brought them to her mother's bed and knelt on the floor between them. I did likewise, sitting off to the side. I told Ann that her mother had shared with me that she had a nice cat named Callie, and asked how she was handling all this upset in her life. "Oh, she's fine," said Ann. "She's at my house with my dog Muttsky. They're inseparable. Muttsky's a Maltese, and Callie and he have been friends for many years, but Callie will make friends with anyone. I brought her in yesterday and she spent the whole day on the bed with Mom. I couldn't bring her in today. I am kind of on a lunch break, but I don't think I am going back."

Suddenly, Dottie began shaking, crying out and moaning. At this, Ann became very alarmed and jumped to her feet. "I am going to get the doctor!" she said. "Please stay with her." I nodded that I would. The look of terror in Ann's face was unmistakable, and I felt almost guilty to be so composed by comparison. Patients and their families come to hospice knowing why they are there and that this is the end for them. Yet, still, the families panic at the sight of suffering or weakening. I had often done just that with my own mother, calling nurses in the middle of a long, worrisome night for support and peace of mind.

When the doctor came in, I excused myself and told Ann I would keep her in my prayers.

About four days later, I came again to Dottie's room. The blinds were open and Dottie was alone, the squirrels feeding contentedly at their banquet. Dottie had mercifully slipped into a peaceful coma, facing the blinds, her eyes open, staring but unseeing. I moved Woody and Katie into a position where Dottie could reach them with her left hand that was hanging from the bed. I didn't think she would react at all, and she didn't. I left the dogs by the bed for a moment, and went to close the door. I came back to her and stood very close to the bed. I bent down and whispered in Katie's ear.

"Where's the squirrel, Katie!"

At this, Katie let out a single woof! Dottie's eyelids flickered slightly, and I moved Katie under her hand. Dottie's hand brushed against Katie's coat in short, almost imperceptible strokes, and I was certain that she knew we had come to say goodbye.

9

But You Cannot Hide

*We can walk the journey for only
a little while, love me while you can*

I T WAS ANOTHER STORMY SOUTH FLORIDA SUMMER
afternoon, and the western sky was a gun-metal blue. Katie,
Woody, and I had not had much luck that day, the patients all
either too sick to talk or not in the mood. It seems that the
weather affects the dying much the same as it does those of us who
are industriously moving through our day. The dark, dreary days
find us sleepy and unsociable, and the bright sunny days find us
with dispositions as parallel as possible under the sad
circumstances of our confinement.

As a result of the weather and the prevailing somber mood, we
were pretty much headed out the door when we passed a room that
seemed to beckon. Without any reason or deliberation, the dogs
took it upon themselves to turn into the doorway. The name on
the door was "Curtis," and I entered very quietly. I was still not
sure why. At first it appeared as though the room was empty. The
bed was unkempt and seemed unoccupied. But something about
the shape of the dishevelment made me tentatively enter the
room and take a closer look.

And, yes, the shape was human after all. An elderly black man was curled in the fetal position. He was completely covered from the very top of his head to his feet by a thin white bed sheet, topped by a lightweight mint-green blanket, all loosely wrapped about him. As I came around the side of the bed, I could see two tired, cloudy eyes peeking forlornly out from underneath this makeshift hooded sleeping bag. I spoke to Curtis, softly so as not to startle him.

"Are you cold?"

He shifted his eyes to meet mine. "No! Why?" His voice was surprisingly strong and defiant.

"Because you are all wrapped up in your bedclothes," I pointed out. He didn't reply and we regarded one another in silence for a moment. "You almost look as if you are hiding," I said with a smile. He didn't answer, so I pressed on. "Are you?"

He looked a little angry at this and I feared I had ventured too far into the private thoughts of a dying stranger. At last, it appeared he had decided to take the high road.

"Well, yes, I guess I am hiding," he allowed. "But there is no way to hide and you can't hide from what I got." He sounded very bitter. Woody and Katie had been standing quietly and hadn't moved at all. He didn't see them. He barely saw me, peeking as he was from his shelter from the storm. Another few awkward moments went by, and I thought that I really should be leaving and give this poor man some peace. Yet, I stayed.

"So, um, Curtis?" I ventured, after a few moments. "Do you like dogs?"

He eyed me suspiciously. "Dogs?" he asked. "Now it seems to me that that's a stupid question. I like 'em all right. What're you asking me a thing like that for?"

With this I brought Woody and Katie into the room. "Well, Curtis," I said. "These dogs are my partners. This is Woody, she's a Lab, and this is Katie, an Aussie, and some people have this idea that they are going to make you feel better. Like they will be calming or therapeutic or something like that." I looked at him expectantly. "So," I asked hopefully. "Do you feel better?"

Curtis looked at me with disdain, and I knew at that moment that I had blown it. My feeble attempt at humor had been ill-advised and I had to admit that I was no Patch Adams. Curtis raised himself up and rearranged his blanket around him. He took a long time assembling the pillow, the blankets, situating himself in an upright position so as to better face me. I figured I was in for it. People who are dying have little time or patience for making nice-nice, and I knew that I was about to be told off in a very big way.

But Katie and Woody didn't see it that way, and they decided that all this activity meant that someone wanted to pay them the homage that was rightfully theirs. So they pushed forward and placed their heads on the side of the bed, nudging his hand, Woody snapping playfully in the air. Curtis looked at them with a frown. "Damn, man," he said, with a frown. "Can't nobody get no peace in this place, anyway? I was minding my own business and now I got this white lady and these dogs and, geez already, wassup with that anyway?"

I was mortified, it was much worse than I had anticipated. I gently tugged on the leads and started to back away. "I am so sorry, sir," I whispered. "I am really sorry. We will leave you alone and I am really sorry."

"Just a minute," he said. Curtis's voice was strong and clear, but kind. "Wait a damn minute. You done got me up now, so just a second. Now you seem like a nice lady, so I am gonna tell you something, OK? Now you got these dogs here and they seem like good dogs and all. But, I want you to turn around right here and look behind you. Now go on, look on that table by the patio. Tell me what you see." I turned around and understood at once why he accused me of asking a "stupid question." There, on the table, were six matted and framed eight-by-ten photos of a most magnificent, majestic, and perfect German Shepherd dog. The photos seemed to follow this beautiful animal through his lifetime, from puppy- to adulthood, and it was obvious that this dog was well loved, well cared for, and part of a very lucky family. All I could say was "wow."

I stared at the photos for a long time. I took my time and looked at each of the photos, gently picking up each frame and studying the picture, carefully replacing them one by one on the table. The first two were of the dog as a puppy, and in one photo the dog was held by a much younger Curtis. Curtis was wearing a police uniform and kneeling down, cradling the puppy with one arm, the other holding the lead aloft. He was smiling proudly. The third picture was of an older dog, wearing a vest and police insignia. The fourth and fifth photos depicted the dog wearing a medal around his neck, and in one he was paired with Curtis and posed in a row of eight other human and non-human police officers, all wearing ribbons and medals. The sixth photo showed the dog sitting in a living room, surrounded by children, as if posing for a family portrait. And there was another item, also bearing a photo, albeit much smaller than the others. It was a beautiful black marble urn, almost a foot high, and topped with a gold dome. I recognized it immediately—as I have the ashes of my beloved Sable in a similar vessel, though not nearly as fancy. And the photo was affixed to the urn exactly as my Sable's was at home.

Woody had resumed her visit with Curtis, who was watching me quietly, petting Woody on her head and stroking her soft ears. Since her target was in a bed, Katie figured the belly rub would have to wait and was quickly falling asleep on the floor. I finished looking at the pictures and turned to face Curtis.

"So," I prodded. "Who is he?"

"*She's* Sgt. Shadow," he said with pride. "And *she* was my partner for twelve years. So, now, you still want to tell me about dogs?" His look was one of feigned arrogance, so I bowed my head like a chastised child.

"No sir," I said. "I think maybe you can tell me a thing or two, yes?"

Curtis laughed at this and took Woody's face in both his hands. He was looking in her eyes, but talking to both of us. "I loved that dog, and she loved me. She would have laid down her life for me if she had to. She almost did, several times. She lived with me and my wife, but my wife never liked her. Said she was my first love and called her a bitch!"

He shouted the last word and we laughed at the obvious pun. "But of course she was!" I laughed. "So, Curtis, tell me, how did you work it out with your wife, then?"

"She learned," he said with a satisfied nod of his head. "She learned that this dog would save my life and she knew that, without Sgt. Shadow, there would be no job for me. I was with the police force out in California for forty-two years, but the only time I really enjoyed my job was the time I spent with that dog." Katie was in a deep sleep, having abandoned all hope of a belly rub, and Woody was leaning quietly against the bed, lazily wagging her tail in response to Curtis's attentions.

I noticed something odd about the table display, and I just had to ask. "Curtis, there is just one thing though, I don't see any wife pictures, only dog pictures. Wassup with that?" I said with a smile.

"She left me long before that dog did, uh huh. She left out of my life and never looked back. She said she wasn't about to share her home with any damn dog. So she left me. And me and Shadow lived in that house alone. She protected me and we went to work every day. When Shadow got too old to work, they retired her, and I left too. I went to work for a security agency and we walked around resorts and construction sites, just me and Shadow."

At that moment I felt a heartfelt empathy and despair for this man's loss. He had lost his best friend when his beloved Shadow passed over, and, not for the first time, I felt despair at the fact that dogs have a life span so much shorter than our own. His pain at his partner's loss was unimaginable, such was the love he still held for her in his heart and soul.

"She died when she was thirteen. She was getting very slow, very stiff. Then one day, she looked up in my eyes and I could almost hear her say, 'Partner, I just don't want to do this anymore,' and she slept the days away. Taking her to the vet to have her put to sleep was the hardest thing I ever had to do. Yes ma'am, it was."

Curtis turned his attention fully to Woody again and told her how beautiful she was. Woody looked into his eyes and wagged her tail in happiness and gratitude. Sgt. Shadow was coming to get Curtis soon, Woody was telling him, probably very soon. He couldn't hide from that.

"I'm taking her with me," he said softly. "I got her ashes there and I told everyone to put that urn in my casket with me. I am making sure they will."

I made up my mind at that instant to do the very same thing one day.

"You know, I almost didn't come in here," I said. "You looked so annoyed and miserable and I didn't want to intrude. But the dogs seemed to want to come in, so I followed."

Curtis looked at me for a while, then down at Woody. He sighed heavily. "Well, I heard somewhere that some people think dogs can help sick people. Maybe it's true, coz I still can't hide from what I got, but I got to be with Shadow again for a time."

"Yeah," I agreed as I knelt to wake Katie. "That's what dogs do: make it better for a time."

As I left the room, a nurse was coming towards me down the hallway. She looked up and saw us coming from Curtis' room and made a face. "You didn't go in there, did you?" she whispered.

"Well, the dogs did," I smiled. "I just followed along. Why? Was I not supposed to go in that room?" I looked at my volunteer briefing list and sure enough, Curtis' room was not listed. "Oh, I am sorry. I do see now he's not on the list. I hope I didn't break any rules, did I?"

"Well no," said the nurse, looking nervously in the direction of Curtis' door. "But he isn't exactly our most pleasant patient and we kind of discourage the volunteers from going in there. Because, frankly, we don't want them getting insulted or, well, abused. Was he awful to you?"

I understood her fear completely. "Well, no, not really," I told her. "He told me about his dog…the one in the pictures. He told me about his job, his wife that left him."

"He had a wife?" the nurse asked incredulously. "Wow! How about that! He never says a word to us. Unfortunately, we kind of avoid him now because he is just so rude and always tells us to just leave him alone."

"I think, maybe you need some resident dogs here at hospice," I told her. "There's so much work to be done."

"Yes," she agreed, still looking in the direction of Curtis' room with awe. "I'll be damned! He had a wife."

10

The White Dog in the Night

I knew you would come,
I always knew you would come

GLORIA'S ROOM WAS TINTED SEPIA IN THE LATE afternoon sun, and was heavy with the smell of urine and vomit. Woody and I were working alone that day, and we almost didn't enter the room. As unpleasant as it was for me, I was sure that Woody, with her sensitive canine nose, would find it just unbearable. But dogs don't think like that, so in we went.

The aura of sickness and death was present in the faint lighting and the powerful smell in the room. Gloria was a very old woman. Her skin was stretched tight over her face and dappled with liver spots. And it was shiny and white as porcelain. Her eyes were clouded over, a deep blue, and baldness showed through wisps of yellow hair. She was laying flat on her back, with her head resting on two pillows, her eyes staring up at the ceiling. She held a pink kidney-shaped bowl on her chest, and her hands were covered with skin that looked like a single sheet of white tissue paper, lined with purple veins and deep wine-colored splotches. As we came around the side of the bed, Gloria shifted sideways to see who had entered her room. It took her a moment to focus, but when she finally saw us, she shouted in amazement.

"It's him! This is the white dog that I see passing my window every day! Oh, I knew he would come to see me, I just knew he would come in and see me!"

Gloria struggled to sit up straighter so as to get a better look at Woody—squirming and wriggling her frail body while trying to keep the little bowl in place.

Gloria looked at Woody again. "Yes!" she cried out. "It's him. You're the white dog that comes by my window every night!" Gloria was ecstatic. She was sure she was being visited by an angel of a dog.

Woody and I didn't have the heart to tell her that this was not possible, so we went along. "Yes, I bring Woody here all the time, and it's possible she was outside your window."

"No, no," Gloria insisted. "This dog has been coming to my window at night. He's been walking past my window every night and even in the day sometimes."

I looked at Woody, who was innocently studying Gloria, obviously fascinated with her excited state and tales of Woody's nightly adventures.

"Well, Woody," I said. "What do you have to say for yourself?" Woody looked up at me and smiled her lovely doggie smile, wagging her tail and looking for all the world the picture of innocence, puppy-like and above suspicion. Dogs keep secrets very well.

"You must love animals," I said. "Have you a companion animal?"

"I did," said Gloria. "I have had animals all my life. I love animals, I just love them. There was one that was really special to me. I used to go bowling with my husband and daughter every Sunday night."

With a nod toward the logo for the Rockies plastered all over her bulletin board, I asked her if she was from Colorado. "Oh yes," she affirmed. "We went bowling even when it was snowing and cold; we never missed our Sunday night bowling league. One night, we came out of the bowling alley and I saw a dog across the street. He was tied to a tree! There wasn't a house around, so I knew that the dog had been left there. It was the dead of winter," she said, her voice rising in indignation "How can anyone do that to a dog?"

I asked her what he looked like.

"A Foxhound type, a mix, he was, a Foxhound kind of dog tied to a tree. Can you imagine?"

I shook my head with mock incredulity. "So, what did you do?"

Woody walked over to Gloria at this point and laid her head on the edge of the bed. Gloria slowly and with great effort brought her hand to Woody's head. "I have been vomiting" she said, "I just keep vomiting. I may have to, so I keep this bowl on my chest." Indeed, the bowl was not empty, so I offered to take it and empty it for her. When I returned, Gloria was speaking softly to Woody who was looking at her with sleepy eyes. "You love me, don't you?

You do. I know that you love me. I love you too." She repeated these words over and over and Woody was taking it all in.

I was reluctant to break the hypnotic spell, so I waited for a while, pretending to be busily cleaning her bowl and drying it over and over with a paper towel. Woody was, once again, working her magic.

"So," I said finally. "What did you do about the Foxhound?"

"Well," she said. "My daughter told me not to get involved. My husband said to leave it alone; he didn't want to get involved. But I told them that they should shut up and help me! I was so mad at them for not being the least bit concerned about this little dog. So I put my stuff in the trunk and ran across the parking lot, jumped over some hedges, and crossed the busy highway to get to this dog. He was tied to a tree by a brand new rope around his neck, and he was shivering. Foxhounds don't have very heavy coats, you know, and he was so cold. It took me forever to get the roped untied. My fingers were frozen and my husband and daughter just stood at the car watching me—never even came to help me!"

"Gee," I mused. "That had to have been hard for you. Did you take him home with you?"

Gloria petted Woody some more, and again began cooing to her. "You love Gloria, don't you? You are just so sweet, how can anyone be so very sweet? You do love me, don't you? You do love Gloria. You come see me in the night. I see you. I know that you are there, I know you come see me in the night." Woody sat perfectly still, her head resting on the edge of the bed. She almost looked as if she were asleep, if it were not for the fact that she was sitting up.

"I did take him home," she said finally. "I named him Murphy. I put signs up everywhere, but nobody claimed him. And you know, that dog loved me too. He loved me very much. He knew that I saved him. Imagine leaving a dog out on a cold winter night to fend for himself, and tied to a tree. Do you know how he showed me his love?" I shook my head, sitting down on the armchair to hear the story of how Murphy loved Gloria.

"Every night, after dinner, I would let him run loose. I would open the back door and let him out to run. He loved to run, and he always came back. When he came back, he always brought me a present! The first time, it was a complete frozen rib roast! I didn't know where it came from. I think maybe someone had their door open and he ran in and swiped it." We both laughed at this and I asked her what she had done with it. "I cooked it and we both ate it, of course! He took the bones and buried them all over the yard! But isn't it funny that he brought it to me to be cooked and didn't hide it for himself? Another time, he brought me home a package of frozen chicken parts. I don't know where they came from. We cooked those too and we ate the chicken. But I didn't give him the bones. You aren't supposed to give dogs chicken bones, did you know that?" I nodded that I did.

"One time, he came home with a turkey carcass, it was soon after Thanksgiving. It was a whole turkey carcass, and I knew he had gotten into someone's garbage."

"Oh dear," I said. "What in the world did you do with that?"

"Oh, I had to throw it out, of course. But I didn't want Murphy to know that. So I took some of our own turkey out of the fridge and cooked it up and gave it to him like it was his. You know, that dog smiled. He did. You can say that dogs don't smile, but I am here to tell you that Murphy smiled." I didn't argue. Hadn't Woody had done just that very thing moments before?

"Wow, that's a great story. I guess that was a long time ago, huh? Do you have any animals now?"

"No, I don't," she said. "I live in an apartment. But when I get out of here I am going to buy a house and get another dog. I love animals. I have never turned an animal away in my whole life. Not any dog, not any cat, not even a gay-co."

"A gay-co?" I asked, uncomprehending.

"Yes, you know one of those lizards with the fat tails. A gay-co."

"Oh, right!" I said. "Where in the world did you find a gecko?"

"When I moved to Florida, I saw a gay-co on my patio one morning. I scooped him up and put him in a shoebox, took him to the pet store. They told me what it was and how to take care of it. I bought him a house, some sand, some crickets. All the neighbors have cats and those little foo-foo dogs. But I can tell you one thing for sure—I was the only old lady in my condo with a gay-co!"

She laughed, as did I; and a funny little picture flashed in my mind of the sweet little old ladies all coming to Gloria's house for their weekly game of Mah Jong and being cordially introduced to their friend's new housemate!

Gloria asked me about Woody, how old she was and how it was that we came to be at the hospice. I explained how therapeutic animals can be, how wonderful the reactions of the patients are, and how the dogs inspire people to think about happier times. I shared with her a story of a tiny African-American infant, all hooked up to wires, who stopped sucking on her pacifier when she saw Woody. Gloria listened for a moment. "That's very nice," she said softly. "You have done her a great service, and all dogs too. You know, when the baby gets better and grows up, she will always love dogs, will always remember dogs. How nice that you showed the baby the dogs!"

I was saddened by the beautiful sentiment, because I knew that the baby wouldn't grow up at all. I kept that secret to myself.

We chatted a while longer and said goodbye. "Woody," Gloria said. "I will see you tonight. I will know your name this time, and I will see you outside my window tonight."

Two days later, I brought Woody back to see Gloria, but she was already gone from this world, and I knew that she was in the company of a dog called Murphy, a little black angel who loved dogs, and a fat-tailed gay-co.

11 ⟿

Alfred and Tilly

It was the Redbones,
they taught us hound

THE VOLUNTEER'S BRIEFING LIST INCLUDED AN unusual notation: "Visit the couple in room 105." I thought it odd that a couple could have been admitted together, and my curiosity took over as we headed in the direction of the room. The notation summoned in my imagination a romantic vision of a loving couple, lying together, hand in hand, drifting toward a final destination. I thought of that scene in the movie *Titanic*—the elderly couple who had simply stayed in their stateroom, awaiting their fate in a loving embrace. I indulged in a little fantasy: "How tragically beautiful, one not leaving the other behind, until death us do part...."

As I neared the room, however, I could hear a heated argument in progress, and I was a full five doors away!

"You always make such a big deal of things," a man's voice was saying.

"Well, Alfred, this *is* a big deal" came a woman's reply.

"I don't know why you have to make a federal case out of every little thing," the man said again.

"Oh, give it a rest, Alfred," the woman replied. "I don't understand why for once you can't see things my way!"

Confused and startled out of the idyllic scene playing out in my mind, I looked at the name on the door of room 105. Alfred. Just Alfred. So it wasn't a dying couple after all, but a dying husband whose dedicated wife had moved in bag and baggage and set up camp in the hospice room. I had heard stories of situations such as this. But this was my first experience with the arrangement that was encouraged by hospice as being therapeutic for both the dying and the loved ones who must be left behind. This, though, didn't sound very therapeutic, and I started to pass by, not wanting to intrude on a quarrel between a married couple. But Woody and Katie had other ideas. They barged in, pulling at their leads, with me vainly holding them back.

The wife was standing sideways, rummaging through a large tote bag on the chair and she saw us first.

"Ooh look, Alfred!" she said. "*Dogs!*" She smiled broadly and rushed to meet us at the door, arms outstretched, reaching for Woody and Katie like a grandmother greeting her beloved grandchildren. The spat was instantly over.

She was an elderly woman, stooped with osteoporosis and moving her abundant body with great effort. She looked like anyone's grandmother, with gray hair nicely coiffed and wearing large white enamel earrings with a necklace to match. She was surrounded by tote bags of every size, shape, and color. Her name, she said, was Tilly.

Alfred, of course, was in the bed. He appeared to be surprisingly strong and vibrant for a hospice patient. "Come in, come in," he beckoned, very much the gracious host. I almost expected him to offer to make me a drink. But Woody and Katie were already in.

"Oh I have nice things for them to eat," Tilly gushed. She stopped and looked at me as if for the first time. "Oh, they can have a little something, can't they?" she asked. I told her how their parents were vets and they were very careful about what kinds of foods they ate, but that I was certain they wouldn't mind a little treat. "Oh that's awful," Tilly said, and made a face. "How can anyone not give them nice things to eat? Dog food is dreadful and unpleasant and dry and all, they should have nice things for their tummies!"

Woody and Katie got solidly behind this effort; they liked where this was going! I agreed, and so Tilly searched through her tote bags, pulling out all manner of stuff in the process. She flung cosmetics and pajamas and tissues and magazines and books and combs and lotions and photographs and postcards and letters. She carefully lifted out an enormous bottle of amber-colored mouthwash, followed by witch hazel, shampoo, and a baggie full of bobby pins. Finally, her hand emerged clutching a somewhat flattened box of graham crackers. The dogs were practically salivating! I could almost hear them say "C'mon already! Make with the cookies!"

"We love dogs," Alfred told me. "We just love 'em. We had dogs all our lives. We always had Redbone hounds. They were the most wonderful dogs. They are so smart and so handsome. We raised them. We had the top show dog in the country back in 1976!" he said proudly.

"Oh Alfred, that wasn't seventy-six," said Tilly, frowning. "It was during the Nixon administration, *seventy-four!*" She looked at me conspiratorially. "He gets a little confused sometimes," she whispered. "It was during the Nixon administration." I nodded that I understood.

"I can hear you!" Alfred said, rather loudly. "I am not dead yet you know!"

Tilly waved her hand dismissively. "We can *all* hear you, Alfred!" she shot back.

As Tilly shuffled through the box of graham crackers, I explained to her that Woody and Katie don't take handouts with much grace. They aren't very gentle, and I was concerned Tilly might nick her hand on an overenthusiastic canine fang.

"Don't be silly!" Tilly said. "They will take nice for me. Watch. Watch me show you how." I was resigned to watch, fearful that a poor little old lady was about to get her hand bitten off by Jaws masquerading as a couple of kindly hounds. But then (Thank God), Alfred summoned the dogs to his side, bribing them with the remains of his lunch.

"C'mere, you dogs. Now, come here and let me share my lunch with you. I have some nice grapes for you."

"Alfred," Tilly interrupted. "Dogs don't eat grapes. They like crackers. They don't like grapes." But Woody and Katie loped greedily to his bed, anxious for any forthcoming bits of food.

"They don't take very nicely," I repeated, wanting to avoid an injury. "Woody and Katie never really learned to 'take nice.' I don't know why. But if you tell them to 'sit' and toss the grapes in the air, they will catch them very nicely. They really like that."

"Well, they are not going to like grapes," insisted Tilly. But Alfred told them to sit, and, of course, they caught the grapes in the air and delighted Alfred, who now had finally, it seemed, gotten something right.

"Who taught them that?" Alfred asked, obviously impressed at the little trick they knew. "Did their dad the vet teach them that?" I nodded that he had. "Well, that's a great little game to teach a dog!" Alfred smiled agreeably.

"Well, they are only eating grapes because they like the game," huffed Tilly. Still determined to show me a thing or two about training dogs, Tilly had finally managed to extract a few shattered graham crackers from the box and called Woody and Katie back over to her side.

"Do you mind?" shouted Alfred. "I was playing with them. They were helping me eat my lunch." But Tilly ignored Alfred's protests and had assumed the aura of a schoolmarm.

Apart from their stellar evaluation as Delta dogs, Woody and Katie are graduates of a dog academy of the highest order. Consequently, they are well trained to sit, stay, lie down, and come. And they do it with such aplomb that the little issue of "taking nice" seems unimportant sometimes. This was not one of those times.

"Now, Woody, Katie. *Sit!*" Tilly commanded. And sit they did. "Now Woody, Katie. *Stay!*" And so they stayed. "Now watch this," Tilly said, looking directly at me. "Watch how I do this."

"OK," I said. "But really I have to warn you...." I was stopped by the look in her eyes. I was defeated; it was really out of my hands.

"First," Tilly began. "You let them see you have something. Like this." She showed them the crackers in her hands, held just out of reach. I waited for the sound of snapping jaws, but Woody and Katie seemed to be enjoying the game and were behaving with patience and grace. I was amused at the idea that they seemed to know they were playing a game, one that they would win in the end. "Then, you just give them a nibble. Like this." Tilly exposed just enough of the crackers, to each dog in turn, to let them nibble just a bit. "And finally, you tell them. 'Take nice, take nice, take nice,' " she cooed as she fed them each in turn small bits of graham crackers. "See!" Tilly looked at me triumphantly. "See! I have a way with animals, don't I? You bring them back tomorrow and I will have more cookies for them and I will teach them again. You be sure to bring them back every day and I will teach them to take nice. OK?"

What could I say except yes?

The following day, we returned to find Alfred had saved several pineapple squares and melon balls and was waiting for us. As I entered the room, I could hear Alfred's voice.

"I never liked that timeshare stuff. You did, you liked it. I never did. You always dragged me off to that...."

"Oh, hello!" said Tilly when she saw us again. "Look Alfred, they came back."

Alfred turned in my direction and smiled broadly. "Hello, hello. Come right in. Bring those nice dogs right over to me. I have some of my lunch here, I was waiting for you." Again he asked them to sit and stay, and again he tossed the fruit in the air as Woody and Katie caught the flying fruit in their mouths, wolfing them down, intently watching for the next offering. Alfred was smitten with Katie especially, who, having no tail, always seems so serious and businesslike. The sight of her catching flying pineapple cubes in midair is comical because of the contrast. And once again, Tilly repeated her lesson with Woody and Katie, all the time bragging about her prowess with dogs. "See, I told you I have a way with dogs. See how nice? See that?" And Woody and Katie were obedient little pupils, playing the game, playing along, winning hearts and graham crackers along the way.

Several days had passed before we were able to visit the nice couple who used to raise Redbone hounds. I knew something was amiss when I looked at my briefing notation and saw, instead of "visit couple," the words "visit wife." My heart was heavy as we headed for room 105, and I longed for the day when I heard sounds of bickering charging down the hall. The room was darkened and I tentatively entered. Alfred was in a deep sleep, Tilly dozing quietly on the loveseat. I stood in the doorway for a moment, thinking back to just a few days ago when I had envisioned a couple bracing for a journey together and finding instead one on his way and one who must stay.

I let go of the leads and Woody and Katie entered the room slowly, sensitive to the palpable change in the room from their last visit. Katie slowly nudged Tilly's knee and Tilly opened her eyes. Seeing Katie, she said sleepily, "Hello darlings. Hello my little darlings. Alfred has no fruit for you today. He isn't eating today." She looked up at me and her eyes were full of sorrow. "I went to the cafeteria earlier. I have cookies for them. In my bag, if you could just get it for them." Her voice was tired and full of resignation. I crossed the room and opened the bag Tilly had indicated. I found the cookies, wrapped in cellophane, and opened the bag. I started to hand the bag to Tilly when she stopped me. "You do it," she said. "I showed you how. Now you do it, OK?" I knew that Woody and Katie had been playing the game with Tilly, and in all the time I had known them, I had never been able to get them to "take nice"—no matter how hard I tried.

I hesitated, but Tilly was adamant that I give it a go. "Woody, Katie, sit," I said. They obliged. I held the cookies in my hands as Tilly had, and showed them to Katie and then to Woody. They knew the drill, and they accepted the cookies gently. "Well, that's amazing," I told Tilly. "I am truly amazed that they learned to 'take nice' after all this time. Where did you get your way with dogs, Tilly?" I asked.

"The Redbones," she answered, and motioned toward Alfred. "They were his dogs. He loved to go to the shows, he had all the trophies, the ribbons. He used to handle them himself. He had a way with dogs. He is the one who taught me. Now I taught you. He was talking about Woody and Katie before he went to sleep.

He told me to make sure you try it yourself. He wanted you to know how, so they would not ever forget what we taught them. He always said that dogs love to learn things. He truly believed that. So it's good that you can keep up their lesson. It's good."

Looking at Tilly, I suddenly saw before me not an elderly wife, but a blushing young girl, fervently impressing her handsome young suitor, longing to show him how right they were for one another. I finally understood why Tilly was so resolute in teaching Woody and Katie to be gentle, why it was important to show Alfred that she could teach them, and why she was so proud of her "way with animals."

She was desperate to prove to Alfred that his teachings, his legacy, his passion for dogs would live on. They would live on because she showed him how she could teach a lesson to two sweet dogs who came to lunch one day.

12

One of a Kind

Do not be afraid,
I am a good dog

WHENEVER I TELL PEOPLE ABOUT MY VISITS to hospice, they almost always express apprehension at the possibility of seeing little children who are sick and dying. Without a doubt, the prospect of visiting a terminally ill child makes it difficult for people to volunteer at hospice. Indeed, there is something "off" about a helpless little baby alone in a stark, sterile hospital room.

One day, Woody and I stepped out of our busy lives and into the room of a dying baby. And yes, I felt the sense of profound sorrow one would expect. The room was bright and cheerful, with colorful helium balloons, bright flowers, and stuffed animals in abundance. There was a confusing mixture of auras; that of a cheerful little-kids' birthday party mingled with the gray, brooding cloud of death. The decorations were necessary, I knew, but still seemed an insult to the tragedy unfolding in the room.

In all the other rooms, the bed is positioned in the center of the room. However, in this room the bed was against the wall, adjacent to the door, not readily apparent upon entering the room. And in this room, there was not a bed, but a crib.

In the crib was a baby. She was lying on her left side, facing out so that she could see the room. Her big, black eyes were wide open, and they were clear and bright. A narrow plastic tube had been inserted in her nose, taped to her cheek, and led to a machine mounted on the wall. The little girl seemed so vulnerable and fragile, wearing only a plain white disposable diaper and a light flannel blanket. The pastel yellow of the blanket was soft and pale next to her chocolate-brown skin. Her arms were curled up in front of her chest, her head resting on tiny hands tucked under her cheek, palm to palm. I could see the wounds of old IV needles. On a table in front of her was an eleven-by-fourteen-inch picture of what appeared to be an enormous extended family. Some caring soul had taken great pains to position the picture so that the baby could see it clearly through the bars on her crib.

As we entered the room, the child did not stir. I moved with Woody so that we could enter her line of vision slowly. So unsure was I of the baby's reaction that I almost held back, not wanting to startle her by the sight of a very large dog. As we came before her, her eyes shifted almost imperceptibly to meet those of Woody. She looked intensely at Woody and didn't blink. The only sign that she had seen us was a cessation of the soft sucking noise coming from tiny lips around the pacifier. Even that simple cessation of movement gave me hope that we had done what we come to hospice to do, give a terminal patient a brief respite from what was happening inside them. But this baby was too young for menacing thoughts, and it was her boredom we interrupted instead.

I watched the little girl stare intently at Woody, who stared back with benevolent brown eyes, and wondered what both were thinking. I was captivated by the incongruity of it all—a tiny baby suddenly seeing, probably for the very first time in her life, a big yellow dog. We stood in front of the infant for a very long time, and I finally emerged from my reverie so I could lay my hand lightly on her back and say a silent prayer for her. How many times had I heard from others that they couldn't bear to see a sick child! Yet here I was, faced with that very image. I felt a curious sense of peace for her, and relief that she would not suffer. And there was something more. I felt deeply privileged for having this moment with her. Indeed, I may have even felt a trickle of envy at this child's imminent flight to the angels of mercy. It was sad, but beautiful too.

I asked Woody to come closer, telling her to come see the baby in the bed. She obliged by placing her nose through the rails, and sniffing gently at the baby, then resting her chin on the mattress. The look of wonder and fascination in the baby's eyes was unmistakable. She continued to hold her pacifier in her mouth but did not make a sound and did not suck. She was altogether immersed in Woody's kind face and understanding eyes. Woody had had some experience with this setting. Didn't she have a little human baby at home as well?

After a while, a woman and young boy entered the room. The woman looked to be about sixty, and the boy about eight. The woman was visibly unhappy to see us there, and the boy was terrified of Woody. When Woody saw them, she wagged her tail and started in the direction of the newcomers, always happy to make the acquaintance of new friends. I had to pull her back gently to caution her to go slowly with this child.

The boy cowered behind his grandmother, and let out a yelp. "Who are you?" the woman inquired, a little *severely*.

"We're pet therapists," I explained. "We came to see the little one here; she seems to like Woody." I introduced myself and asked the boy if he was frightened of dogs. He nodded warily that he was. "She's very friendly," I told him gently. "She would not hurt you at all. She's very sweet. Don't you think you would like to pet her?" I asked.

He looked at his grandmother for some clue as to what she would have him do. "He's afraid of dogs," she said. "His next door neighbor had a big dog, a pit bull. Bit him; got him right on the leg. So he's afraid." I could not read the look in her eyes. She seemed to be daring me to dispute her statement. She was a substantial woman, a woman who looked as though she ruled her roost without challenge. I wasn't sure what to do next.

"I am so sorry that happened to you," I said to the little boy. I asked Woody to lie down, trying to make her smaller than she was, so as to keep the boy comfortable. The baby, having lost Woody from her view, had resumed her sucking with a loud "*sluurrrpp*" and we all looked her way. "Is this your grandchild?" I asked.

The woman sized me up and apparently decided that I was one of those annoying cheerful do-gooders, totally oblivious to insults, and therefore harmless. Her attitude softened noticeably.

"Yes, my daughter's her mother, but she died of AIDS." She nodded toward the infant. "Angela was born with it. Now she's dying, too." The woman joined me by the crib and began to tenderly caress the baby's head. The boy was glued to her side.

"And this little guy is my grandson. That's his baby sister in the bed," said the grandmother. I was relieved that the little boy appeared to be the picture of good health. He was a tad overfed, and freshly scrubbed. He wore Nike shoes and a shirt, and his pants were, fashionably, much too large for him. I was overwhelmed with compassion for him and his grandmother. They had certainly been through some very sad times. I admired her for her strength and courage in the face of all that was happening, and told her so.

"Well," she sighed, noticeably softening at these words of commendation. "God don't never give you no more than you can handle, I know that. We've been coming here for a week, just sitting in this room, visiting. It's been hard on him. He gets bored," she said, indicating the boy who was still cowering behind Grandma.

"But this large family. It looks like he has a lot of cousins and friends his age," I said, indicating the photo.

"Oh, that was at Angela's christening. Those people all live outside the state—most of them in Georgia, some in South

Carolina. We're the only ones that live around here. So it's just me and him come to visit every day."

"I'm very sorry. We were just paying a little visit, saying a prayer," I said to the grandmother. I looked at the boy. "Listen. I know you are afraid of dogs, and I don't blame you. Being bitten is a really scary thing, right?" The little boy nodded. "What's your name?" I asked him.

He shrunk back farther behind his grandmother, never taking his eyes off Woody, who was now snoozing on the floor. I was grateful that Katie had decided to stay at the office today. Two big dogs would have been far too much for the child to handle.

"Tell the lady your name," said his grandmother.

"Ben," said the boy, still looking at Woody.

"Well, Ben," I said. "I would really like to introduce you to Woody. Do you think you would be OK with that? Because she likes you a lot, and I think it hurts her that you are afraid of her. She would never, ever harm you. Maybe you could just shake hands with her, OK?"

Ben looked up at his grandmother again. She looked me directly in the eye and asked me if I was sure that the dog was OK. I was happy to explain to her about the certification Woody had been through, and how she goes to the schools and participates in all kinds of children's programs. "Well," she reasoned after hearing the explanation. "Maybe it wouldn't hurt to take his mind off of his momma and sister. Go ahead, now, Ben," she said to the little boy. "The lady says it's a nice dog, goes to see the children in the schools. That dog ain't gonna hurt you, it's OK."

Ben came out from behind his grandmother and looked at me expectantly. I called to Woody, who was awake and had been listening to me talk about her. "Woody, sit." Woody was the picture of disciplined obedience. I took a position on the floor, kneeling so as to be eye-level with Ben. "Ben," I said. "I would like you to meet my friend Woody," and I gently pulled him alongside of me, so that we were both facing her. Woody stood still as a statue, her mouth open in a relaxed doggie grin, her tail wagging lazily behind her. "Woody, shake," I suggested. Woody put her paw up in the classic "shake paw" stance, and Ben stepped back a little. I gently reached for his hand and, laying his small hand atop mine, we shook Woody's waiting paw together.

Ben smiled. I expected a show of apprehension, a little fear. But if Ben felt that, he didn't show it. He smiled in delight and Woody gave him a kiss on his cheek, which made him drop to the floor and giggle. At this, Woody stood up and wagged her tail joyfully, licking Ben and offering to shake hands again. I sensed that maybe Ben really wanted to like dogs after all. He just needed to meet the right dog.

"See!" I exclaimed "See how nice?" Ben's grandmother was smiling at Ben and told him that not all dogs were bad dogs, people had to make them that way. "Most dogs are nice dogs," she told him.

"Can I hold her?" Ben asked me, reaching for the lead in my hand.

"Of course," I said, and handed him the lead. "But where do you want to take her?"

"Well, where do you go?" Ben asked me. I told him about the visits to the patients' rooms, and asked if he wanted to visit the patients. He looked at his sister doubtfully and said he didn't think he wanted to do that. I had an idea.

"How about we go to the cafeteria, and you can wait outside the door with Woody while I go in and get us all some cookies?" Ben's grandmother nodded in agreement as she took her seat next to the infant's crib. As we entered the hallway, Ben proudly walking beside Woody, a nurse came along and, seeing Ben, exclaimed: "I see you have a dog today! Did your sister see that big dog?" Ben beamed proudly and said that she had.

"We're going to get some cookies," Ben told the nurse.

"Oh, today they have oatmeal-raisin," the nurse told him seriously. "You'll have to get two for that big dog. She looks like she likes to eat lots of cookies."

Ben and Woody led the way and the nurse and I walked together a few feet behind. Ben began to skip down the hall, with Woody happy to trot alongside. "We all know Ben," said the nurse. "He was here three months ago to be with his mother. Now his sister is here, too. It's so hard on him, sitting there with his grandma all day, never having another kid around. I feel for his grandma, too. She's been stoic, but I know her heart is breaking. The two of them are in that room from the time he gets home from school until late at night, only leaving to get take-out. This is really great for him; this is a good idea."

I told her how Ben was so afraid at first, not wanting to come out to meet Woody, about how a pit bull had bitten him, causing him to fear all dogs. "That's sad," said the nurse. "Better make sure you remind him that even though Woody's a good dog, not all dogs are good dogs, because I would hate for him to go back to his street and go up to another pit bull, thinking it's OK when it's not."

"Gee, that's right," I agreed. "I didn't think about that. I must remember to tell him that not all dogs are like Woody."

Woody is one of a kind.

13 ⮎

Rx for Pain

He is my therapist,
my friend, my love

THE BRIEFING LIST DOESN'T ALWAYS INCLUDE notations next to patient room numbers, and I generally take that to mean that either the patient and family do not want to be disturbed, or the patient is comatose and therefore unable to appreciate a visitor. As we approached the doorway to room 114, I saw that it was unlisted and started to pass by. A woman in the room saw us pass and caught up with us in the hallway. She was one of those women possessed of simple classic beauty, with blue-black hair heavily streaked with silver and pulled back in a long ponytail. She wore no makeup or jewelry except a basic slender, gold wedding band, and a watch with a silver and turquoise band. She was dressed in a long, full denim skirt and silk purple blouse. She had the serious look of a scholar, and she reminded me of primatologist Jane Goodall.

The woman told me that she had seen us walk by and asked if we were pet therapists for everyone or if we were there to see someone in particular. Her face was full of pain and anxiety, and I gently explained about the room number being unlisted. "Oh," she said, nodding her head in understanding. "We've only just arrived this morning. I guess we came in after the list was printed. I'm Sarah. Please come in, we really love dogs." Woody and Katie and I turned and followed Sarah into the room.

The gentleman in the bed was Sarah's husband Jack. He was a distinguished gentleman, with gray hair and handsome features. He didn't look all that sick to me, yet he grimaced in pain and fidgeted, as if trying to find a comfortable position. Jack squinted at my name badge and, reading it, said my name in greeting. "And who are these guys?" he asked me, nodding at Woody and Katie.

"My partners," I said. I was about to introduce them when we were interrupted by a nurse who appeared at the door. "Jack? Are you feeling any better?" the nurse inquired. "Did the medicine kick in at all?"

"No, ma'am, it did not," Jack answered, somewhat apologetically.

Being that the primary focus of hospice is to make the patient as comfortable as possible, pain management is a really big deal at hospice. I have often heard the patients conversing with the doctors and nurses, as my own mother had, using an uncomplicated numerical "pain scale." They give the pain a rating on a scale of one to ten, ten being the most intense. Jack spoke in that language now. "I'm afraid it's still at an eight right now. It's down a little, but it's still not gone."

"Oh, I'm sorry," said the nurse. "The pain medication I gave you an hour ago really should have kicked in by now. I can ask the doctor for some more if you like, but it may take me a while to find him." Jack closed his eyes and his face contorted in pain again.

Sarah spoke for him. "Why don't you do that?" she asked. "I think he really needs something more." The nurse agreed and hurried from the door.

"He's uncomfortable," Sarah said to me, quite unnecessarily. "Oh, I'm sure," I said. We stood in silence for a few moments, not sure how to proceed. Sarah spoke again. "You know, we have a dog that looks a lot like that one," she said, indicating Katie. He's a tri-color Border Collie. She's an Australian Shepherd, right?"

"Yes, she is," I affirmed. "I was about to tell you, this is Katie." Katie looked up at Sarah as if to say hello. "And this is Woody, she's a yellow Lab. And I love Border Collies as well. Well, I mean, I love all dogs, but Border Collies are very smart. Isn't that the dog in *Babe?*" I asked, attempting to make small talk while poor Jack was writhing in pain on the bed.

Sarah looked anxiously at Jack, who attempted a brave smile. "Isn't there anything we can do for you?" she asked him.

We. She had said "we." Sarah didn't want to be alone with her helplessness. She wanted company. We had been pressed into service, in this together. I wanted so much to be of some help, some use. I looked at Woody and Katie, but they appeared to be as uninspired as I was. My mind raced back to a painful moment in time when my mother-in-law was beset with cancer and in excruciating pain. She had asked us to stand beside her and elevate her right arm. Inexplicably, this simple act brought her some relief, and family members took turns at her side, holding her hand high in the air. I wondered if Jack needed a similar change of positioning. I offered this to Sarah.

"You know. Maybe it would help to be sitting up. Should we try getting him to the loveseat? Would you like that, Jack?" Sarah asked.

Jack answered: "Who knows? Whatever. Maybe. OK, I think that may help." Finally, he nodded in agreement. I asked Woody and Katie to "down, stay" and stepped outside to look for a helper. I found an orderly and he returned with me to the room. The three of us assisted Jack to the loveseat. He sat at one end, and, for reasons known only to her, Katie jumped up to be next to him, curling, circling, and decisively fitting in beside him. She often did this in the car, taking her "shotgun" place while Woody was relegated to the back seat. In all my time with these two, I have learned that Katie is, without a doubt, the alpha dog.

In any event, Jack was obviously delighted at Katie's behavior and commented on how bold she was to have taken the best seat in the house. Sarah helpfully covered them both with a light blanket and then took a seat on the bed, and I on the chair. Woody settled in, leaning against my chair. Jack had put his arm around Katie and was petting her slowly, telling her how fine she was, how very sweet she was, what a very beautiful girl she was. These are the moments in a dog's life that I think make them wish they could purr. For, if they could, Katie would have been doing so at that moment.

"I have a dog that looks like you," Jack told Katie. "But he's not as pretty as you. No, he's not. He's a handsome dog, but you are the prettiest dog I ever saw. My dog's name is Frankie. He's a smart dog. He likes to go on my boat with me, and we take long walks." At the word "walks," Woody looked up and Katie's ears perked up and she looked at him, head cocked to one side. Jack laughed and said he was really sorry for saying the "W" word.

"Frankie does that too," he said. "He knows all the words, doesn't he honey?" Sarah had reclined back on the bed and was propped on her elbows.

"Sure does," she smiled. "How are you feeling?" Her face was still a study in extreme anxiety.

"I don't know," Jack said. "But Katie looks pretty comfortable."

Jack continued to tell Katie about Frankie—how old he was, where he came from, what he likes to do. All the while she was looking intently at him, perhaps hoping for another word she knew, perhaps just thriving on the soft sounds of his voice, enjoying the petting and being the center of attention. I had dropped to the floor with Woody and we were sitting together, relaxing in our own friendship.

"Tell Katie about how Frankie likes to play with the dogs on the beach," said Sarah. At the word "beach," the dogs once again became attentive and alert. "Oops," said Sarah. "Now I did it. I'm so sorry, girls. I didn't mean to get your hopes up." Sarah and Jack exchanged stories of Frankie's puppyhood, and all the while Jack was stroking Katie and talking softly to her. She looked like she understood—not the words, of course, but Jack's need to refocus his attentions on something other than his intense pain. She was ever so happy to be of service!

After a while, the nurse returned. She had a glass of water and a small paper cup containing pain medicine. She was surprised to see Jack on the loveseat. "You're out of bed! I have your pain medication here. But, gee, you look like you are doing better. Are you?"

"I guess the medicine did kick in after all," Jack said. "I think now maybe it's down to about a two."

"Thank God for that," said the nurse. "Let's get it down to a zero." And she gave him his medicine and water while we waited. "It will make you a little sleepy, but you will be much more comfortable," she said, and was gone.

"Thank Katie for that, I should think," said Sarah. Jack brightened at this and readily agreed.

"That's right," he said. "Thank Katie."

We talked a little more and, after a while, Jack surrendered to the twilight haze of his pain medicine and asked to be brought back to bed. With great effort he bent down and gave Katie a light kiss on her head. "I love you Katie," he told her. "You made me feel better."

Sarah walked out the door with me and thanked me again. "I think I may run home so that when Jack wakes up he'll have Frankie there with him," she told me. "I had no idea that being around animals can be so helpful. Too bad they can't prescribe dogs for pain," she said sadly.

Watching Katie just being Katie filled my heart with pride and gratitude for the wonderful beings we call dogs. Be it physical or mental, spiritual or imagined, dogs are, without a doubt, timeless healers in fur coats.

14

Time to Walk the Dog

*Do not break the sacred
and mysterious covenant. Do not.*

I CONFESS I HAVE HAD MANY AN OCCASION WHEN I reined in my emotions listening to a dying man reminisce about having been a hunter who brought down his prey with dogs. The sight of Woody invokes these stories because Woody, being a Labrador, looks like a dog that many have pressed into that gory practice. And once there was a man who had been a butcher, and the butcher's wife was there as well, and my tormented, self-righteous, *animal-activist self* found it so hard to keep still while my caring *volunteer self* worked compassionately well with dogs who are unconcerned about such matters. Like the time Jesus fought with Satan in the desert, my body is the holder of two beings: the competent defender of the defenseless in bitter combat with the humble angel of mercy.

But there was this one time....

Woody and Katie and I had not been to hospice in over two weeks, and, when we finally came together again for our outing, we were full of wanton joy at our being together. Our visits on that day were all quite routine and normal—a friendly hello here, a kindhearted hello there. We were simply happy to be together!

We bustled into Richard's room to find a fortyish man in bed, bandages about his arms and neck, sleeping quite peacefully. On the loveseat beside the bed was a middle-aged couple, who waved us in.

"Does anyone here like dogs?" I asked—my customary greeting that got right to the point.

"Oh yes!" said the man on the loveseat. He was a very red roly-poly man with a pink roly-poly wife. "I like dogs!" he said. "But my wife is afraid of them."

I looked at her, concerned that we may be causing her some discomfort, and asked her if she wanted us to go. "No, it's OK," she assured me.

"We had dogs, too. So did Richard," said the man, beckoning Woody and Katie to him by clapping his hands. They immediately obliged.

"Oh, that's great," I said, happy to be among dog people, "What kind?"

"Oh, they were Cocker Spaniels—two of them."

"Nice dogs," I said, nodding pleasantly.

"Yeah. I was always afraid of dogs, but then he got those Cockers and I let them sit on my lap and sleep on the sofa, and I got to like them a little too," said the wife. She was looking at Woody and Katie, but not reaching out to touch them. "We had to put 'em away when we moved down here. That's my brother in the bed. We moved here a year ago to take care of him and the place we moved to didn't take dogs."

I couldn't believe what I had just heard, and although the smile remained frozen on my face, the rage inside me was ascending from the pit of my stomach and seizing my heart and soul.

"Wait," I said cautiously. "Put them away? You mean you had to put them down?"

"Yeah," the man said, much too matter-of-factly. He was still petting Woody and Katie and I wanted to run across the room and steal them away from these ghastly people who "put dogs away."

I decided to delude myself into believing that they put them to sleep because they suffered horribly from some dreadful disease and humane euthanasia was the only choice they had. I mean, really, what choice did *I* have? I was, of course, there to lend comfort and support to grieving patients and families.

"I am so sorry to hear that," I said, managing a sympathetic smile. "I guess they were too old for new homes, right? How old were they?"

I held my breath.

The answer came back: "Eight."

I knew in my poor fractured heart this was little more than middle age for a healthy Cocker Spaniel and felt a deep sense of shame and pity.

"We didn't want to do it," the man said.

Oh no, I thought. Had he read my mind?

"But we were in an awful hurry to get down here, with Richard being so sick and all. And we had to take the first place that was available. We had no alternative." The couple both shook their heads, remembering back to what was undoubtedly a tragedy for them and their little Cocker Spaniels who slept on the couch.

The experts all say that pet therapy works so well because dogs are loving and non-judgmental. It's true. Woody and Katie had not reacted at all to this unsettling news. They were happy to lend their affection to this man.

I felt a peculiar mixture of *anger* at a society that allows landlords to discriminate against family members without so much as a stirring of rebellion; and *pity* at these poor people who believed they had no other option. The fusion of these two feelings was disquieting.

A strange, garbled sound came from the man in the bed. "Is it time?" The words came from deep inside a heavily drugged sleep. Richard was talking in his sleep. "Is it time?" he repeated.

We all looked his way, and Woody sauntered over to investigate. "He's waking up," said the woman. "I am so glad he's going to get to see the dogs now," she said happily. "He had a Cocker too, but we had to put him away when he moved in with us at the apartment."

Good God! Another Cocker Spaniel dead. "Was he old?" I asked hopefully.

"Dunno," said the woman, "about ten I guess."

I will be honest. I was not managing this well. I needed to leave. My spirit was broken and I wanted to get Woody and Katie out of there. Put away indeed! I started to make some excuse about getting the girls back to their loving and protective family when Richard awoke and sat up in the bed.

"Is it time?" he said, looking from Woody to Katie, and then to me.

"Time for what?" I asked him, but I didn't want to know.

"Time to walk the dog?" he said. He swung his legs around the side of the bed and, with great difficulty, placed his feet one by one on the floor.

I looked at the roly-poly couple on the loveseat and waited for their reaction. They were looking at him with all the interest of couch potatoes watching a rerun on television.

"What does he want to do?" I asked them.

"He wants to walk the dog, I guess," said the woman.

I walked closer to Richard and helped him into his robe. "Do you want to help me walk the dogs?" I asked him.

"Oh, it *is* time!" he exclaimed.

I handed him the handle of Katie's lead and he started out the door in his stocking feet. Woody and I were close on their heels. We came alongside him and Katie when we got into the wide hallway.

"I used to walk my dog every morning, and every night when I came home from work.," Richard said. "She had a doggie door for when I wasn't home. We used to go for three-mile walks early in the morning and just after suppertime. I brushed her every day and all the neighbors loved my Brandy." I listened quietly, trying to comprehend how anyone who loved Brandy so much could allow her to die.

"When I get out of here I am going to take her for walks again. She kept me going after I got sick. I really miss her. I'm so glad it's time to walk the dog again. Who's this dog?" he asked me.

I was very confused. "That's Katie," I said flatly. I didn't get it. So the couple in the room didn't tell him that Brandy was "put away"? I had to try to understand.

"Where is she now?" I asked Richard, who looked at me questioningly. "Brandy," I clarified.

"She's here," he said, looking at me like I was daft. "She's right here," and showed me Katie's lead.

"Right," I said. I looked at Katie who had been marching along like a trooper, leading the way like the alpha dog she is. She was looking back at me as if to say "Hello? What's the hold up back there?"

We walked around the hospice in silence—through the hallways, into the atrium, doubling back along the wings of the hospice. We were greeted along the way by nurses and visitors who wanted to chat, but were ignored by Richard and Katie who were plodding along. I smiled helplessly at the ones I made eye contact with, but couldn't stop to talk as I truly needed to keep up.

"Well, girl, that was a good walk," Richard said. "Guess we need to head back now." He looked at me and asked where we were supposed to go. I stopped a minute and looked around, trying to get my bearings. I looked down one hallway, and then the next, and finally saw Richards' roly-poly sister and her roly-poly husband standing in a doorway.

"Oh, it's this way," I said, and started off in the direction of Richard's room. Woody and I led the way back.

When we arrived back at the room, Richard handed me Katie's lead and thanked me for helping him walk the dog. "Katie, you say her name is? Well, bye Katie," he said. Shrugging off his robe, he resumed his position on the bed. I stood in the doorway trying to sort out the events that had just happened. The couple was still in the hallway, chatting with the visitor from a neighboring room. I came up behind them, dogs in tow.

"He says he's going to see Brandy again when he gets out of here," I told his sister.

"He gets a bit baffled sometimes," she said. "When he moved in with us, we tried very hard to get the landlord to let us bring Brandy with him. We even got a note from his doctor. But nothing worked. We didn't really have much money, so we just had to put her away. We told him she was going to live with the pet sitter. I mean, we couldn't tell him the truth; it would have killed him right there."

I nodded in sympathy, and truly felt it this time. I was furious with a nameless, coldhearted landlord and thought again at the schism within a society that treats their animals like family members yet tolerates killing them because of inconvenience.

I didn't know quite what to do with all this rage. I said goodbye to the roly-poly couple and headed off to the cafeteria for some cookies for Woody and Katie so we could sit quietly for a moment in the atrium before going home.

I needed a little pet therapy myself.

15

Hooray for Hollywood

Music hath charms to make
the dog take a nap

THERE ARE SOME DAYS WHEN I LEAVE HOSPICE feeling very good about being Woody and Katie's chaperone and the metaphorical wind beneath their furry wings. But there are also days that I leave the facility with the unsettling realization that life can sometimes be very unfair. While most patients are compelled to tell stories of their own companion animals whom they loved along the journey, Woody was the catalyst for one patient who took a path less traveled down the road of reminiscence.

It was another of those legendary stormy South Florida summer afternoons, and even the building itself was lethargic. The patients, for the most part, were asleep. And the staff members, for all their dedication, were a bit humorless. It was a blah day.

Woody and I were working alone that day as Katie had fallen victim to the mood as well, indulging herself in lazy, satisfying snoozes. We signed in at the volunteer desk—Michelle Rivera and Woody Berkenblit, here for pet therapy, time 1:15. I glanced over the briefing list and told Woody that today was to be an abbreviated visit. Previous experience had taught me that patients are sleepy and non-communicable on days blessed with what Floridians like to call "liquid sunshine."

The first few rooms we entered were serene and quiet, with sleeping patients as well as visitors. We decided to try just one more room and then call it a day. The patient, Rita, was sitting up in bed, gazing off into space, lost in her own imaginings. She was an old woman, with startlingly wild red hair and bright green eyes. She would have been considered statuesque had she not been lying in a bed, and she was thin, though not painfully so. She was, I'm sure, a knockout in her day. She saw us as we entered the room.

"Hello," I whispered. "We're volunteers, we just came to say hello."

Rita looked at me and smiled faintly. "I'm Rita," she said. "I'm really sick."

"I know," I said with a sympathetic smile. "Is there anything I can do for you?"

"Yes," she answered. "You can get me some cold water, and maybe open the sliding door just a little. I love the smell of rain."

"Oh, so do I," I told her truthfully. I was happy to have a chore to do, and I asked Woody to sit still for a moment while I took the plastic pitcher to the cart just outside the door so that I could fill it with ice. I refilled the pitcher with fresh water, and poured a cup for Rita. She took it gratefully. "The rain has slowed to a drizzle," I told her as I crossed the room to the sliding patio door. "But there's a nice warm breeze and the fresh smell of rain is still in the air." I opened the door a few inches, and walked back over to where Woody was waiting patiently, watching my every move.

"I love the city in the rain," said Rita. "I love Manhattan all the time, but especially in the rain, it makes the whole world so fresh and new, and clean. So clean. And the grass in Central Park turns all shiny green. It covers the rocks and makes them all polished and black. I love to be in the city when it rains."

Having spent time in New York City recently, I understood.

"I see your name on your name tag, but I can't read the tag on your little friend here," Rita said, looking in Woody's direction.

"Woody," I told her. And at this Woody wagged her tail in greeting. "Her name tag is attached to her collar, but you can't see it from there."

"Woody? But you said 'her' tag. So she's a girl dog?" said Rita.

I get this a lot.

"Well, she's not my dog, you see. She's my partner. I really never knew why she was named Woody. I know her mom and dad are Woody Allen fans. So I always thought that was why," I said.

"Oh I do love Woody Allen movies," said Rita. "He's one of my favorites."

"Me too," I agreed. "But it turns out that's not the case at all. Adriana, she's the hospital administrator at Woody's parents veterinary clinic, she told me that her real name is Hollywood, and that we just call her Woody."

"Hollywood? Really? How odd," mused Rita. "I never heard of a dog named Hollywood before."

"I know," I laughed. "Me neither. I guess that's why we call her Woody."

Rita took a sip of her water and struggled to sit up straighter. I assisted her in plumping the pillows behind her and fixed her blanket so that she was covered and comfortable.

"Woody," Rita called. Woody came to be beside the bed. "I want to sing you a song."

And with that, to my sheer delight, Rita began to sing.

"*Hooray for Hollywood,*" she started out very low and gently, "*that screwy, ballyhooey Hollywood!*" She struggled to make her voice heard. "*Where any office boy or young mechanic, can be a panic, with just a good-looking pan.*" She smiled at us and Woody wagged her tail, happy to be the center of attention. Rita continued her singing, her voice getting just a little stronger, her eyes dancing to the orchestral music playing in her imagination, "*And any barmaid, can be a star maid if she dances with or without a fan, Hooray for Hollywood!*"

I was clapping to the beat and Woody was taking it all in.

Rita paused. "Why don't you sing along with me? Don't you know the words?" she asked.

"No," I admitted. "Do you know all the words? I didn't think anyone really knew all the words to that song!"

"Well I do," she said proudly, and continued where she had left off.

"*Where you're terrific if you're even good! Where anyone at all from Shirley Temple, to Aimee Semple is equally understood. Come on and try your luck, you could be Donald Duck! Hooray for Hollywood!*"

I was laughing now and Rita was too. Woody was also enjoying the fun. "Donald Duck?" I proclaimed. "That's not really in there is it? And what in the world is a good-looking pan?"

She answered by singing even louder: "*Hooray for Hollywood! That phony, super Coney, Hollywood. They come from Chilicothes and Padukahs with their bazookas to see their names up in lights, all armed with photos, from local rotos, with their hair in curlers and legs in tights. Hooray for Hollywood! You may be homely in your neighborhood. Still, if you think that you can be an actor, see Mister Factor, he'd make a monkey look good! Within a half an hour you'll look like Tyrone Power. Hooray for Hollywood!*"

"What!" I said, laughing. "Who's Mr. Factor and why's he got a monkey?" I asked her. We collapsed in paroxysmal laughter but Rita laughed so hard she started to cough and I was fearful we may have gone too far in our gaiety. After a moment, she composed herself and I offered her some water, which she took gratefully.

"Max Factor, the cosmetic guy, he can make a monkey look good." She answered my question. "Wow," I said. "I'm all for good-looking monkeys. And I have a dog named Tyrone. My mother told me that there was a movie star named Tyrone Power, but I didn't know he was, you know, like a big celebrity or anything. And really, the words to that song are, well they don't make any sense. It's a nonsense song, right?"

Rita looked at me in feigned disgust. "Tyrone Power was *the* leading man back when I was a young girl. But with Loretta Young and Alice Faye around, who could compete?" She threw her hands up in mock surrender and smiled. "And," she leaned in and whispered, "the words to the song make some sense if you're in the business."

(I thought it best not to mention that, although I certainly had heard their names, I didn't *really* know who Loretta Young and Alice Faye were either).

"Were you in the theater?" I asked.

"Oh yes, I was. I was in an off-Broadway show once, but my singing career never really took off. I became a music teacher instead, teaching private piano and voice lessons until I retired here in 1989." She looked at Woody, whom I wish I could say was raptly listening to the story, but who had, in reality, curled up to take a nap after the singing had stopped and the conversation was no longer about *her*.

"So why didn't you sing along with me?" she asked me. "Music is the universal language of the soul, you, know. Don't you like to sing?"

"I love music, but I guess I don't know the words to that song. I didn't even really know there were words to that song. Sorry, guess I should have pretended a little, huh?" Rita laughed at this and asked me what song I did know the words to. I thought for a moment, trying hard to bridge this generation gap, searching my memory for a song that would span the ages and would be a song we both knew well. My mother must have been listening from her place in heaven because, at that moment, I had an inspiration. I looked at Rita playfully and, with great inhibition, began to sing "*Start spreading the news...I'm leaving today....*" She joined in with me and together we sang: "*I want to be a part of it—New York, New*

York." Rita reached for my hand and we swayed with the make-believe beat. "*These vagabond shoes, are longing to stray, right through the very heart of it—New York, New York! I want to wake up in a city that doesn't sleep, and find I'm king of the hill—top of the heap!*" At this, we raised our joined hands to the ceiling, causing Woody to jump up and shake off her nap.

"What's next?" I asked her. Though I knew the words by heart, I was still a little embarrassed to be singing them aloud in a hospital with a dying ex-off Broadway star, who resembled Lucille Ball had she lived to be eighty-three.

"*These little town blues, are melting away,*" she prompted. "*I'm gonna make a brand new start of it—in old New York,*" we sang together joyfully. "*If I can make it there, I'll make it anywhere, It's up to you—New York, New York!*"

We heard the sound of feeble applause coming from two nurses and a chaplain who had been attracted by the singing and were watching quietly from the doorway. "What's going on here?" said one nurse. "This isn't music therapy day!" She was delivering a mock scolding.

"No," I agreed with her. "It's dog therapy!" And Rita and I, still holding hands, buckled in laughter at this private joke.

"Dog therapy?" the chaplain asked. "The dog sings?" he joked.

"You had to be there," Rita told him. "It's just one of those things."

"Well," teased the other nurse. "I'll not be having these shenanigans on such a gloomy day."

"Oh really," said Rita, and she gave me a wink. "What songs do *you* know?"

And we all laughed again at the silliness of it all. "Oh no," said the nurse. "You have your victim, you aren't fooling me." Rita looked at the chaplain. "Nope," he said, and turned away. "All I know are hymns—not exactly your speed right now." The other nurse took a few steps back, and then she, too, was gone.

I looked at Rita who was still holding my hand. "That was a lot of fun," I told her. "I am so happy to have made a new friend."

"Me too," said Rita. But the moment was awkward and her eyes were sad. We said goodbye and I promised to bring more song ideas with me the next time I came to visit. We both knew that the swan song we had just sung together was like a falling star, at once there and gone in an instant, a flicker of time never to be repeated, and I mourned for the funny friend I'll never have.

"Woody Herman," said Dr. B. when we returned to the clinic and related the story. "She was named for Woody Herman, a jazz musician from the forties that Lisa and I were into at the time. Woody Herman and his Woodchoppers."

Oh.

It's a good thing I didn't know that when I visited Rita. What on earth would we have talked about?

16

Peaches and Flo, Where Will They Go?

Together we will make it through the night, set your mind at rest and let your spirit take flight

LYING IN THE BED LOOKING SO FRAIL AND forlorn, Jeremiah was the picture of loneliness and despair. He was a very little man, and looked to be at least ninety. His head was covered with a light dusting of fuzzy gray hair. He had no teeth that I could see, and his face was covered with liver spots and purple blotches. He was lightly dozing when we came in his room, and opened his eyes when he heard the jingle of Woody's tags. I was startled by the sheer blueness of Jeremiah's eyes. They were the color of the clear blue sky on a summer afternoon, and they seemed out of place in such an old and wizened face. On his chest, he held eyeglasses and it appeared he had been fiddling with them just before he gave up and closed his eyes. When he saw us, he attempted to replace them, but a lens had fallen out and he began struggling with trembling hands to pop it back in. But his hands were shaking much too hard and he seemed to have trouble seeing what he was doing, what with his glasses off. So his efforts were frustratingly useless. It took me a moment to realize what he was attempting. But when I did, I offered to help him fix his glasses. He gave them to me thankfully.

I worked the lens carefully until it was seated back in the frames, and then cleaned them with Woody's bandanna. Handing them back to him with a smile, I said, "Good as new!"

He took his glasses from me, thanking me, and replaced them on his face. When he did so, he affected surprise as if seeing Woody and Katie for the first time. "Well, how do you like that?" he joked. "There are dogs in my room!" Woody and Katie were watching us and waiting for me to give them a cue that they were to do something, anything. Dogs are really good about that—just hanging out, waiting to be asked to do something for us.

Jeremiah asked me to re-fill his water cup so he could have some water. When he had finished drinking, he thanked me, and finally asked about Woody and Katie.

"Well," he said. "So I guess you're going to tell me why there are dogs in my room?" More surprises! This man whom I had taken for a sad, lonely old man had the bright eyes of a young man and was full of charm and humor.

"Well, they are therapy dogs. They came here today to cheer you up. We thought you might like that. But, of course, you have to like dogs. So do you like dogs at all?" I asked.

Woody and Katie looked at Jeremiah hopefully. Woody wagged her tail in an effort to show him what a lovely dog she was. Jeremiah took his time looking them over carefully, as if assessing them and examining them with great solemnity. But the dogs seemed to know that it was all in fun, and Woody took to snapping at the air as she does when she is happy and being playful.

"I do," he finally said. "I like dogs very much. In fact, I used to raise them. I had Bernese Mountain dogs. Do you know about them?" Somewhere deep within my heart a wish made a lifetime ago and long forgotten sprang to life. When my sister Kerry first started showing Newfoundland's, she took me to my very first dog show. We strolled around the fairgrounds, seeing this dog and that. They were all beautiful, but the one that captured my heart was a Bernese Mountain dog. The benevolence in the eyes of that magnificent animal stayed with me all my life and I only saw it again when I met Woody and Katie.

"Yes!" I said with pleasure. "They are beautiful dogs. I love their handsome intermingling of colors, their luxuriant coats! Oh, and they have such sweet faces! And their eyes, so loving and kind. I never really knew what their personality was like, but I have to say I always had a fondness for them from the first day I ever saw one."

Woody and Katie were absolutely certain I was talking about them, so I just let them believe it. After all, I may as well have been, and said as much to Jeremiah.

"Oh yes, I agree, they some nice dogs you got there. Lemme get a closer look, bring them closer." I coaxed Woody and Katie closer to the bed, and Jeremiah reached a wavering hand through the bed rails. I was, once again, relieved that the dogs were tall enough to reach the bed. Jeremiah petted them each in turn, and Woody rewarded him with sloppy kisses which he didn't seem to mind.

"Where are y'all from?" he asked me, still petting the dogs. "Village Animal Clinic, over in North Palm Beach," I told him. He brightened noticeably and told me that his granddaughter Jennifer worked for a veterinarian in that very same town, but he didn't think she was bringing dogs to hospice. She did, however, help out a couple of cats once.

"There were these two cats, and their owner had gotten very sick and the guy's daughter brought them to the vet hospital for boarding until the guy got better," he said. "But then, the guy died, see, and the cats were still there. So they were going to have to put the cats to sleep. Jenny came over and told me about it, she was in tears. She didn't want them to die, ya know? So I said I'd take them. Now I have them."

"How long ago was this?" I asked him. "Oh I guess it's been about five years now," he answered, and gave a heavy sigh. The irony was not lost on either of us. These were lucky cats to have had this sweet man take them into his heart and home, but now years later, they were inevitably facing the very same fate for a second time in their lives.

Jeremiah spoke up again, "Kinda funny, huh, me being here and them at home and Jenny's probably thinking she's back to where she started five years ago!"

"Oh," I said brightly, "she's not going to let anything happen. After all, they're family now, right? I mean, it's different. She'll take them home with her this time."

"She wishes she could, but she couldn't take them the last time because of where she lives, and she still lives there. No pets.

So I don't know what will happen. They are really nice cats, I like them a lot. One's a calico, really pretty, and the other is a tabby. They are good cats, they really are."

"Oh that's really too bad," I said sympathetically. I raced through my mental list of everyone I knew on the entire planet whom I hadn't already pressed into service at one time or another for the sake of a disadvantaged animal. I wondered what Dr. B. would say if I offered to bring them back to our clinic. I knew that was out of the question. What would we do with them? Absolutely, out of the question.

"I can take them!" someone said brightly. Then I realized to my chagrin that the words had burst forth from non other than my own self. Woody and Katie looked at me like I had lost my mind. But it was too late. Jeremiah smiled as broadly as possible for a man with no teeth. He was hoping for a miracle, and instead got a sucker on the heels of eight furry paws, which worked just as well for his purposes.

"Well, I thank you!" he declared. "I do. I have been lying here worried sick about those cats. I ask my Jenny every day about them, she says they aren't eating without me. She says they miss me something terrible! But when I ask my Jenny about where they will go, she just tells me not to worry about it. But I knew she was bothered. I knew she didn't have no place for them! I was worried sick."

I smiled feebly and tried not to think of the reception this news would bring back at the office. I knew that if I explained how hopeless this poor man was, Dr. B. would understand! How could he not!? I left my card with Jeremiah and told him to have Jenny call me as soon as she could so we could arrange to pick up the nice calico and tabby from Jeremiah's house. He promised he would and we said goodbye. "You girls be nice to my cats, OK?" he yelled to Woody and Katie as they moved out the door. He was grinning ear to ear, not a care in the world.

I never said a word when we got back to the clinic, and Woody and Katie kept my secret safe as well. I knew that when Jenny called, I would have to confess my offer to rescue two ten-year old despondent cats, but I wanted to put it off as long as possible. After all, ten-year-old cats are not easy to place, and we would have to work a genuine miracle to find them suitable homes. But we had done so before, and I knew everyone in the clinic would be helpful when they learned of the situation. They were just that kind of group.

Woody and I went back to see Jeremiah after a few days passed and we hadn't heard from Jenny. I was relieved to see a young woman in his room. I introduced myself and Woody, and, shaking my hand, Jenny thanked me for leaving my card. Jeremiah was in a deep sleep from which he was not to awaken. Jenny told me that he had slipped away just after telling her about how I had offered to take his kitties. It was as if he had some unfinished business to attend to, and with the matter of the cats settled, his spirit's worldly tethers were broken and released.

I sat with Jenny and asked her about her job. As Jeremiah had told me, she was working at a veterinary clinic as a dental hygienist. She had been with them for many years, and was obviously proud of where she was working. We talked "shop" for a while, discussing differing aspects of veterinary assisting and the emotional highs and lows that came with the job.

"So, about these cats," I said. "I guess you'll want to bring them over. But if you want me to come get them, I can do that too. I am sure you will have a lot of arrangements to make for your grandfather. You'll be busy."

"Not really," she said. "We don't have any family. It's just us. We are all the family we have. Well, I guess it's just me pretty soon. I really wish I could keep the cats, like keeping a part of him with me. They are all I have left."

Jenny had been petting Woody slowly, and she had been keeping her emotions in check. But now she let them loose in a flood of tears all over Woody's neck. She was a tiny woman, with long dark hair and Jeremiah's clear blue eyes. Jenny wrapped herself around Woody, as the children usually do, and spent her anguish in Woody's fur. Woody had been seated and was now embraced by this brokenhearted woman. Woody, as usual, stood stoic and strong. I waited quietly for Jenny to complete her "therapy," then spoke up again.

"Your apartment complex or management or something won't let you have them? Even with these circumstances? Surely they would understand. Can you ask them?" I asked.

"Well, it's not exactly true that they won't let me have them," she said. "There is a limit of two cats, and they must be indoor cats, but I can't afford the pet deposit. They want $200 each cat. I simply don't have it. Grandpa didn't have any money, so I have to use whatever savings I have to give him a proper send off."

My heart leaped. I was out of my self-imposed predicament after all. Dr. B. was himself a veritable pussycat when hit up for money. Coming up with $400 was much less complicated than finding a home for two elderly cats. And hadn't he always told me he wanted to find ways to reach out and give back the community!? I would have cheered out loud had it not appeared disrespectful with a man dying right there on the bed! The problem was solved: Jeremiah could die with a happy heart, the cats were saved, and Jenny could keep what was left of her family together. Her cats were coming home with her. I explained to Jenny that I thought maybe we could help her with this. She was reluctant at first, but when I told her it was for the benefit of the cats, how could she refuse? After all, I reasoned, we were not asking for her, but for the animals. How could she not let us help? And I did promise Jeremiah that I would look after his cats. I insisted. Jenny's gratitude was overwhelming as she accepted and she thanked Woody and I profusely. "Hear that Grandpa?" she said, "Peaches and Flo are coming home with me!"

They say the hearing is the last to go when a terminally ill patient slips into a coma, so I believe Jeremiah was listening and his spirit, thus satisfied, quieted itself and knew peace. Peaches and Flo were to be with him soon enough. But for now, they were safe.

An hour later, Jeremiah drew in a very long breath, and was gone.

17 ⟳

Kids and Dogs Club

Is there anything more as it should be
than good boys and happy dogs?

I AM ALWAYS DISCREET WHEN VISITING A PATIENT'S
room. It is, after all, the exquisitely private space of a stranger.
I am afraid of entering and finding the patient in a state of
undress or on a bedpan. Or I could be interrupting a person's very
last moment with a loved one. So I make it a practice to walk by
the room, discreetly peeking in while I do so, so that I may subtly
assess what may be going on inside without disturbing anyone.

One day, there was a little boy sitting on the chair opposite
the doorway, so that he was facing the door at the precise moment
Katie and Woody and I strolled by. He was a chubby little boy,
around ten years old. He had short brown hair, cut in crew-cut
fashion, and was wearing a gray and white striped polo shirt and
khaki pants. He was freshly scrubbed, the way kids always look on
"picture day" at school, or at their First Holy Communion or their
grandmother's eightieth birthday. His elbows were resting on his
knees, his chin in his hands and as he looked up we made eye
contact. In an instant his eyes lit up at the sight of two large dogs
passing by. It must have seemed a little incongruous, the presence
of two big dogs in such a sterile environment. At least, that is what

I read in his eyes. His pleased reaction was my invitation to stop in and say hello.

There was a man I took to be his father seated on the loveseat opposite him. He, too, was resting his elbows on his knees, cheek in one hand, his face turned toward the patient. His eyes were red and swollen. He was also dressed up, wearing an ill-fitting suit that appeared to be a little too tight. His hands were callused and stained, the hands of a worker, a mechanic perhaps—most definitely the hands of a man who worked very hard for a living. The patient was an elderly man, obviously the eldest member of this tri-generational gathering. He was unconscious, and it was apparent there was a deathwatch in progress. I introduced myself and Woody and Katie, and stood very close to the child. I had the sinking feeling that my unexpected appearance somehow embarrassed the boy's father who had been caught by a stranger openly crying, unable to control his despair. I was sure that I had when he abruptly jumped to his feet and introduced himself as Greg, hastily wiping his face and forcing a grin. The child told me his name was Christopher, and asked if he could pet the dogs. I brought Woody closer to him, and Christopher reached out a tentative hand and gingerly petted Woody.

"I have a dog just like this, only black." He looked up at me and smiled happily.

"How old is your dog?" I asked, relieved to have found an excuse to stay in the room with them. I have learned that the longer I stay in a room, the more pronounced the effect the dogs have on the occupants, as the people begin talking to them, petting them and relating stories of their own animals.

"She's two," said Christopher.

"Woody is eight and Katie is nine," I said.

"So what's your dog's name?" I asked.

"It's Pele; named after my favorite soccer guy," Christopher told me.

"Well, Woody's named for some musician guy, and my dog Tyrone is named after a basketball guy. Do you like basketball?" I asked.

"Not really, but I like to play soccer with my dog. He runs around and kicks the ball at me, and we run all over the yard with it. I keep him from getting the ball through the goal; he pushes it with his nose. He really does know how to play soccer. He does, doesn't he dad?" With this, Christopher looked at his father.

"Yeah, I guess." His father smiled a tired smile. He looked and sounded so drained and worn out. He crossed the room to his seat and sat down. Leaning forward, he signaled for Katie to come over by him. I let go of the lead and Katie hurried across the room to greet him. While Christopher and I sat on the floor with Woody between us, he told me many stories of having fun with Pele and his soccer friends. As he relived each little story, his voice rose in excitement and animation. He seemed to be getting happier. So I was stunned when, suddenly, Christopher threw his arms around Woody's neck and hugged her, draping his entire body around her! His body began to shake, so intense was his sobbing. Woody just took it. She never moved. She didn't even appear to be in any kind of distress!

I was caught off-guard and wasn't sure what to do, so I simply let Woody do her job. I was deeply moved by this unexpected release of emotion, and realized I had tears in my eyes. I looked over at Greg who was looking at his son sadly. He simply continued to pet Katie. He didn't move towards his son, he merely allowed Woody to be the therapist, such was his confidence in her canine ability. His eyes were tearful too. Katie finally dropped on her back and exposed her tummy for him to rub. Before long he was on the floor with her, absorbed in the rich tapestry of colors in her healthy, abundant coat. I drew closer to Christopher and put my arm around the little boy.

"Dogs can be so cool, can't they?" He nodded in agreement, still holding Woody tightly, and sobbing softly. "They just seem to understand everything and they just want to be there for you, y'know?"

After a while, Greg asked me about Katie, if she liked to chase balls or play.

"No way, not Katie," I told him. "She just likes to flop over on her back and get belly rubs, unless she is eating." But something profound had happened with Woody and Christopher and it was not easy to make small talk afterward. The change in the room was tangible and it was difficult to tiptoe around it.

Christopher, finally cried out and spent, straightened up a little and offered a weak, embarrassed smile. A moment later, a hospice worker came in and, seeing Christopher with Woody, smiled broadly and greeted both dogs by name. "Oh, this is so nice that they are here!" she said. "But listen, I was coming to tell you that we have a children's club, and I see the therapy dogs are here and that is very important. Take your time and enjoy the dogs. I love those dogs; they're such nice dogs, aren't they?" And with a wave of her hand and turn of her heel, she was out the door, with a happy "See ya later alligator." (We say that a lot in Florida.)

The awkward spell, thankfully, had been broken. So, like anyone does in the company of a crying person, I reached for a box of tissues and offered one to Christopher. He took it and blew his nose. Woody gave him generous kisses and made him laugh out loud. She nipped in the air like a snapping turtle—that little idiosyncrasy she has—and Christopher was delighted with this unusual habit.

I thought he might be feeling embarrassed about crying in front of me, so I told him a story I knew about a cowboy and his horse. "You know what?" I asked him. He didn't look up. "I heard a story one time about a mean old cowboy who frightened everyone because he was so scary looking, what with his dirty face and big hat and all that. Plus, he had patch on his eye, and he was all grumbly and cranky. His voice was rough and he yelled at all the other cowboys a lot. But he had this wonderful horse. He was a speckled horse, with brown freckles all over him, and his name was Lance. The cowboy loved Lance an awful lot and stayed with him all the time. He truly loved the horse that he had raised from a foal. And then, one day, Lance got really sick and the cowboy called the horse doctor, but the doctor couldn't do anything for

him and Lance died. Do you know what the cowboy did?"
Christopher still didn't look up, he had resumed petting Woody
who continued to sit by him, wagging her tail slowly, smiling in
that doggie smile way. "He cried," I told him. "He cried because
he loved his horse Lance and all his cowboy friends saw him cry
and they gathered around him and hugged him and stuff like that.
They weren't afraid of him anymore either because they saw that
he was just like them, just normal like them. So that's the story I
read."

Christopher looked at his dad, who told him that he had
heard that very same story too, and that it was probably true.
After a moment or two passed, I took a deep breath: "Maybe I
should go ask that lady that was just here if dogs are allowed at the
children's club. Wouldn't you like that?"

He looked at me with surprise. "Yeah!" he said, delighted that
the attention was no longer on him. "I think they should have
dogs there," he said, warming to the idea. "Maybe we can play
soccer with them."

"Well," I said, offering Woody's lead to Christopher. "Why
don't we go ask her together?" I looked at the father, who nodded
his head and got to his feet.

"How about I keep Katie here a while, OK?" he asked. Katie
was still in her belly-rub position, so I agreed that Katie would like
that. As I followed Christopher and Woody out of the room, I
turned to his father. He was back on the floor, stroking Katie,
whose eyes were half closed, and who didn't even notice.

We walked down the hall together and Woody led the way. Of course, we stopped at the cafeteria for the cookie du jour, and brought the little plate to the atrium to enjoy them. There was still one trick Woody knew that Christopher had not seen.

"Watch this," I said. "Woody, sit. Woody, stay." Woody eagerly complied, knowing sugar cookies were in the offing. I broke the cookie in pieces and tossed them high in the air, one by one. She caught them all, not missing a beat. I invited Christopher to try it too, and he did so with sheer delight, tossing bits of cookie in the air for Woody to catch perfectly in her mouth.

"Wow! She'd make a great keeper," he said, using a soccer term for goalie.

"Oh, yes," I agreed. "She's definitely a keeper."

Yes, she is.

18

Therapist to the Therapists

Come calm my spirit
and still my pounding heart

I
N THE WORLD OF THOSE WHO STAND ON THE
threshold of the other side there are no absolutes. There is
nothing that passes for conventional, and everyone comes to
this place with their own angels and demons. This is the time for
assessing one's life and preparing for one's journey to the other
side. For some people, this is a time of watchful waiting, silent
evaluation, and bidding farewell to all the people and animals they
have ever known. But for others, it's a tormented time of denial
and rage. There are medicines to help heal the anxiety, and
helpers to fend off the loneliness and fear. But sometimes those
helpers descend the depths of despair and hopelessness. The
question in circumstances like these is who will bring them out?

The tension in the lounge of the south wing was palpable,
though it was not immediately evident why this was so when we
joined the nurses and orderlies who were standing stiffly at the
nurses' station that particular day. We had been visiting the rooms,
dipping in and out of doorways, and were about to stop in on the
lovely dog-loving patient in room 114 when Nancy, the day nurse,
stopped me. She was just entering the room.

"Don't go in there," she said, rushing past me brusquely. "Please, just go somewhere else." Her voice was strained and her face was a mask of fury.

I quickly maneuvered Woody and Katie away from the room. Nancy's behavior was uncharacteristic, and I was confused by her expression. Another nurse beckoned to me and we hurried to her side. "The lady in that room isn't doing well," she whispered. "We think it would just agitate her if you went in there." I was stunned. I had just been in that room three days before and had found a most pleasant young woman who had a family of Pekinese dogs she loved to go on and on about. I was looking forward to seeing her again and talking about her dogs. I gave her a puzzled look.

"Hmm, that is so strange," I replied. "She loves for me to visit and talk about her Pekinese dogs." The nurse looked at me as though I had lost my mind.

"You are kidding right?" she said. I read her nametag before answering.

"Well, no, Jennifer," I said. "But I wonder if we are talking about the same woman. I get confused with the different wings in the hospice, I might be thinking of another room. Is this a young woman? A pretty blonde? And her husband brought her dogs in to see her?"

Jennifer looked at me with bewilderment and then suddenly a flash of insight crossed her face.

"Oh I think you mean Joanie. Joanie isn't here anymore," she said matter of factly.

"Isn't here?" I asked. "You mean she died?"

Jennifer nodded affirmatively and offered a sad smile. "She was a nice lady, wasn't she?" she said.

We remained quiet for a moment longer while I thought of the nice lady with the little Pekinese dogs. She was so young; it was hard to believe she had gone so soon.

Suddenly, a blood-curdling stream of obscenities pierced the impromptu mini-memorial taking place outside the door of room 114.

"I need to get the hell out of here! I want out of here! You can't keep me here! Get me the hell out of here. I don't believe this crap, I don't believe you can do this to me! Get me a doctor!" The woman in 114 was shattering the peace and quiet of the hospice. Woody and Katie closed their mouths and stood staring in the direction of the bellowing. They were on alert because something was terribly wrong in this usually peaceful place of happy endings and oatmeal-raisin cookies. They didn't understand what could cause someone to be making such a racket. Woody pulled hard at her lead, the initial spell of confusion having broken, and was straining in the direction of the angry cries. She had a certain "dog to the rescue" look about her.

The bellowing continued with more demands of liberation, threats to sue the hospice, and insistence in speaking to whomever was in charge. Jennifer and I stood with the orderlies, waiting for an idea as to how to handle this terrible agitation.

"The patients are very anxious," explained Jennifer. "And sometimes the disease destroys their ability to reason or even recognize where they are. They get very violent and act out. It doesn't happen often, and usually the anti-anxiety medicines work really well. But not always." She was sympathetic and I marveled at how kind she was in the face of all this abuse. "I feel sorry for them," she continued. "After all, think about when someone we love dies. It's hard because we are losing someone that we love, but for them, they are losing every single person they have ever known and loved. It's really hard for them."

We could hear Nancy's voice now. "Mrs. Stark, please. Please try to calm down so that I can talk to you. You need to take the medicine, it will make you feel much better."

"No, *dammit!*" came the obstinate reply. "*No! You are not going to drug me! I demand to see the person in charge. Who is your supervisor? Get him in here now!*" The screaming continued until finally Nancy rushed back out of the room and sat down hard on the sofa in the lounge. She was livid. The orderlies and Jennifer exchanged worried glances, but did not go to her. They seemed afraid of her.

Nancy sat on the couch, her face buried in her hands and her elbows on her knees. Her long chestnut hair covered her face like a shroud. We waited. She didn't move. Katie looked from Nancy to me and I dropped her lead. She sauntered over to Nancy and nudged her hands. Nancy looked up abruptly with a harsh look in her eyes. She was about to push Katie away, but when she touched Katie's ear, instead of pushing her out of the way, she stopped herself and then slowly began to pet her. We all stood still for a very long time. I kneeled down by Woody and was petting her, and the orderlies began to busy themselves with their chores.

Jennifer took a place on the floor next to me and was also petting Woody. The raging coming from inside the room did not stop.

Nancy had been crying. "I can't help her. I don't know how to help her. I can't make her do what she needs to do." Katie kissed her lightly on her chin and cheeks, and Nancy responded by stroking Katie with more intensity and she didn't say anything more. Katie flopped down on her back, and Nancy slid down off the sofa and joined her on the floor. She gave Katie the well-deserved belly rub and was rewarded with a look of adoration.

There was nothing to be said or done. Katie had the situation well in hand and was absorbing Nancy's frustration like a big furry sponge. In time, Nancy's emotions became stable again, and she took a tissue from her pocket to wipe her eyes. She petted Katie for a while longer, quietly drawing strength and serenity from her brown eyes and silky coat. The metamorphosis was unquestionable. Nancy had come out of the room an angry and discouraged caregiver, but a few moments with Katie had restored her strength and resolve. She straightened up resolutely and took a deep breath. She looked across the room at me. "It's a good thing you guys were here at just the right time. I was ready to throw something!"

The yelling continued and we both looked in the direction of the room then back at each other. We were smiling at the absurdity of it all.

"You do the best you can," I said. "You always do the best you can. But you know what they say; you are only human. Only a human with human limitations."

"Well then, we need to get you on the payroll," Nancy said to Katie as she playfully roughed up her coat. "We need to get you here for stress management training. We all could use a little of what you have," she teased.

"Just keep her in cookies and belly rubs and she will do whatever you ask," I told her.

Nancy looked up at the door of room 114 and rose to her feet. "Guess I better go back in there. Thanks for letting me escape for a while on your dog," she said.

I went to Katie and told her what a great job she had done with the nurse and that sometimes it's not the sick person who needs a hug but the healers. And to whom do they turn if not another healer?

One with a coat not of white, but of fur.

19 ⁓

The Rehabilitation of Maxine

To know the road ahead,
ask those coming back

I T WAS NIGHTTIME AT HOSPICE. THE SUN HAD JUST graced South Florida with an orange and purple sunset that exploded with brilliant color. Several hours south of us in Key West, I knew the sunset veneration that took place every night on Mallory Square was still being celebrated. But at hospice, the moment had slipped by unnoticed by those engaged in the business of dying and us, their entourage into that other bright light.

Katie and I were working alone that day, Woody having been pressed into service by Dr. B. as a demonstration dog for a television program on the care of the canine ear. Woody was very good at being very good and tolerated this well. So Katie and I were sitting together in the atrium, surrounded by poinsettia and the lights from a Christmas tree and Menorah. We were waiting for the dinner hour to be over so we could visit the rooms without the unnecessary distraction of food. Did I mention Katie is a food hound?

A woman and her teenage daughter entered the atrium, and the girl sat down across the room from us. The mother kissed her fondly on the forehead and then smiled at Katie and me before continuing on her way toward the patient rooms. The girl looked at us and smiled as well, then looked down at the floor, seemingly lost in her own world.

Katie looked up at me, her face full of questions. She was wondering why we weren't talking to this girl. "Is that not why we are here?" she seemed to be saying. I decided to give the girl a little space and time, hoping she would come over and say hello. An elderly couple entered the atrium and came over to greet Katie and ask questions about her. We were happy for the company and spoke to them for quite a while. As they turned to leave, the couple saw the girl sitting on the bench opposite us. She had been watching and listening to our conversation. As the couple left us, they passed the girl and, once behind her, turned to stare.

I guessed she was somewhat aware of the surreptitious, amused gazes she has undoubtedly learned to endure. Maybe that's why she looked the way she did. Gothic. I think that's what the kids call this look. Gothic, a word Webster defines as "…..characterizing desolate or remote settings and macabre, mysterious, or violent incidents." A little out of place in hospice, perhaps, but I hoped her style was more a statement of the fashion of the day rather than an outward display of how she really felt inside.

She was a large girl, made larger by the extreme clothing she wore. She was of Hispanic descent, with ink-black hair and deep brown skin. Her round face was marred by the scars of teenage acne. Her short hair was heavily gelled in no particular order all over her head, with bursts of red, green, and blue streaked throughout. She wore a leather dog collar, prickled with menacing chrome spikes, and her ears were pierced five on each side, and decked out with heavy chrome studs. Her bracelets were also black spiked dog collars, one on each wrist. Her nails were painted black. Her blouse was black on black plaid, short sleeved and buttoned high. Her pants were olive-green tartan plaid, elasticized at the calf, and covered with zippers and pouches and pockets. The ensemble was held up by bright green suspenders. She wore black combat boots, with heels and soles four inches thick, that made her much taller than she already was. Her purse appeared to have been made from the remains of an old purple shag carpet. She was an original.

Katie didn't notice any of this, and was still pulling at her lead in her quest to make a new friend. So I gave in and we crossed the atrium to introduce ourselves to Jody.

"My partner here seems determined to make friends with you," I smiled as we approached. "Do you mind if we say hello?"

Jody brightened noticeably and took her purse from the bench next to her, placing it on the floor to make room for me to sit by her. I introduced Katie and myself and she did likewise. Katie sat in front of Jody and placed her head on her lap, inching closer and closer until she was pressed firmly against Jody's legs. Jody laughed and began to pet Katie quietly, not saying a single word. Katie was in her glory.

"You seem to have a way with animals," I ventured. "Do you have any at home?"

She didn't say a word, she simply nodded that she had.

"Was that your mom before?" I asked. Again, not a word, simply a nod.

"She visiting someone here, is she?" I pressed on.

"Yeah, my dad," said Jody. It was evident there was a great deal of sadness in Jody. I wanted her to share, but didn't know how to open the door without being intrusive on a young girl's private misery. I left it up to Katie, who always seems to know just what to do.

Finally, Jody spoke again. "My dog looks something like her," she said.

"Oh, is she an Aussie too?" I asked brightly.

"No," she said. "She's a mix. She came from the shelter, the one shaped like a big egg."

She was referring to a humane society in West Palm Beach that was built in the 1980s to be truly hurricane proof and a safe place for animals who are turned away from the Red Cross shelters. It was comprised of three big white dome-shaped buildings, hence its nickname, The Dome. It was well known for its extra-special dogs—especially those who had been abused or neglected. I was very pleased to hear about a second-chance dog.

"I know that one," I told her. "They do nice work there. What's your dog's name?"

"Maxine," Jody answered. She never looked at me, but focused solely on Katie, rubbing her ears and gently caressing her face with both hands. Incredibly, for once, Katie did not execute her standard drop-and-roll so that she could enjoy a forthcoming belly rub. She seemed to know that our visit was, for the moment, tenuous and that she still needed to work some magic on this girl to gain her trust. The belly rub would have to wait.

Just then, Jody's mom joined us. She had been crying and was pressing tissues to her eyes. She sat beside me for a while in silence, collecting her thoughts and trying to calm herself. Katie sauntered over to her, and placed her head in her lap. Jody's mom began to absentmindedly pet Katie. Finally, she introduced herself to me and apologized for her outward display of grief. I nodded that I understood. She looked over at Jody. "I'm going back in to see Dad. Come in when you are ready. Jody, we will work through this. We will get through it. I'll see you in the room. When you are ready. Take your time. You love dogs. Take your time."

And she stood up, said goodbye, and left us alone once again.

Katie returned to her place in front of Jody who resumed petting her. Unable to be patient any longer, Katie finally dropped to the floor and rolled over on her back for the belly rub that was sure to follow. I slid to the floor to sit by her, and Jody followed suit.

"I am really sorry you have to go through this. I know it's hard. It's never easy losing a parent. I am sorry for your loss."

Jody nodded and told me that, while she was going to miss her father, it was her mother she was really worried about. "She cries day and night," she said. "I can hear her. She cries all the time."

"I'm sure she does. It's especially hard around the holidays," I told her. We sat in silence a few moments longer and then I asked her to tell me more about Maxine.

"Well," she began. "When we got Maxine, she was only about a year old. She's black and gold, and the people at the Dome said she probably had some Shepherd and Golden, maybe even some Collie. She has a long nose like a Collie, and long hair; but she has ears that stand up, like a Shepherd, and a black nose. When we first got her, she wouldn't come out from under the coffee table. We have a big round coffee table and she would just stay under there all the time. She refused to come out. She shook a lot, too. She seemed afraid of her own shadow. The people at the Dome said she had been abused. When they got her, she was real skinny and scared. She had a rope around her neck that was so tight they had to cut it off, and she bled. They said she had probably been beaten too, the way she cowered when everyone came around."

As it had done a thousand times before, my heart broke at this story. I never harden to these tales and still feel that familiar pain in my chest. But Jody hadn't heard them over and over, and, to her, the story was still shocking and evil—made worse for the fact that it was the life story of someone whom she now loved deeply.

"That's a hard thing, rehabilitating a dog who has been beaten down. I really feel bad for her. It's good that your family took her in. What happened with her?"

Jody continued her story, all the while rubbing Katie's belly and stroking her long silky coat.

"Every day, when I came home from school, I would get under the coffee table with her. I would just get on the floor and reach under there as much as I could. I'd pet her and talk to her really nice. She'd come out and let me put the leash on her, and I would take her outside, and then bring her back in. She'd always run right back under the table. So, I would just get under there with her and talk to her and pet her. Finally, one day, when I brought her back in, she ran to the table but didn't go under. She stayed right by it, and I sat with her. We played tug with the rope toy, and she started to wag her tail. But when someone came home, she would go under the table again. She only came out when I was alone there."

"That is so wonderful that you gave her your time and attention to help her," I said. "How long did this go on?"

"It took about three months. I did this every day when I came home from school, and then I would spend the night playing with her, and she finally started sleeping on my bed with me. My mom didn't like it at first, but I told her we needed to do whatever it took for Maxine to feel comfortable with us. So she gave in."

"That's very cool," I said. "So what is she like now?"

"Oh, she's great!" Jody smiled a truly beautiful smile. "Now when I come home from school she runs to greet me and she's wagging her tail and she's really happy to see me. We spend a lot of time together. She's my dog now."

"I am glad you were able to work through that tragic beginning with Maxine. So now she'll be returning the favor and helping you and your mom work through what's going on with your dad," I said.

She looked at me, bewildered, and suddenly the light of understanding came through her eyes.

"Oh, right!" she said. A revelatory moment. I shared with her the story of my Tyrone, who came to me and helped me through a similar loss.

"Maxine will be a good friend for you. Keep her close to you. Like Katie here, she just wants to help."

"I will," she said. She rose to her feet to visit to her dying father. "Thanks."

It looks as though Maxine has her work cut out for her. But she's more than up to the task, I'm sure.

Every dog has her story. Sometimes, the story never ends.

20 ⤚

A Children's Festival

*It is time to send in
the hospice hounds*

OMETIME DURING THE HOLIDAYS, HOSPICE
plays host to the children who have been participating in a
bereavement support group. Pulling out all the stops,
therapists of every persuasion come forward to help the children
who have lost a parent or grandparent or will lose someone in the
very near future. There is the music therapy department with their
variety of musical instruments for banging and blowing and
strumming. There is a clown, and a baker of gingerbread houses. A
nurse becomes the purveyor of cotton candy, and a doctor the
master of spin-art. A social worker paints butterflies on the faces
of children, and everywhere there's food and ice cream, bean-bag
babies, and yo-yos.

It is only natural that Woody and Katie be present at this
holiday gathering to offer their special brand of therapy as well.
Nowhere are their therapeutic talents more evident than when
they are working with children.

My first impression upon joining the festival was that never
had I ever been to such a large gathering of children that was at
once subdued and festive. The contradiction was palpable and

unsettling. Here was a clown, there was a sad child. Here was a giver of bean-bag toys, there was a downcast child submissively accepting the prize. By the decorations and festive food, one would expect boisterous voices and happy shenanigans, but there was a troubling quietude. If one didn't know this was a children's bereavement group, one would simply recognize that there was something very wrong, and wonder at its cause.

As is usual, when we first come into a setting, it took a while for the children to come to Woody and Katie. They were both freshly bathed and smelled like that wonderful soap and candle store in all the malls across America. They wore shiny new collars decorated with holiday buttons and bows. The first child to say hello was a beautiful little toddler name Nicholas. His mother held him in her arms, where he buried his head in her shoulder. She looked worn and tired, and my heart went out to a young mother who was coping with a dying loved one and a toddler as well. Did Nicholas ever sense his mother's abject weariness?

She placed him before Katie and showed him how to rub his hands in her luxurious coat. For a while, he simply stood at Katie's side, holding himself upright by standing close to her. He watched his mother closely. After a moment, he began to dance to the beat coming from the music therapy room. He danced and danced his heart out, all the while holding on to Katie's back for support. He bobbed up and down, and twirled around. "That's his happy dance," his mother laughed. "He does that when he's excited."

Dogs have that effect on people.

A little girl came over to greet Woody. She was about ten and was pale and thin. She took Woody's buttery ears in both hands and immediately buried her face in the space between them and spoke softly to her, telling her how pretty she was. I asked if she had any animals at home.

"A Siamese cat, but she died," she said.

"I had a cat once, too," I told her. "She died three years ago. But do you know I still cry over her when I think about her?"

She looked at me intensely. "You do?" she said.

"Oh yes. I cry a lot whenever I think of her for too long. She was my love."

"I cried when my cat died, too," she said. "But it wasn't that long ago. I still miss her. I forgot about her...." Her voice trailed off, as if remembering. "Yesterday, in group, the lady asked everyone if they ever had anyone in their family die before," the little girl continued. "I said no, but I forgot about my cat. I forgot how I felt when my cat died. When someone else in the group said that she had lost her grandmother, the lady asked her how it made her feel and how she worked through it. But I didn't think I lost anyone, so I couldn't really join in. But now I just remembered that I did lose my cat, and that was someone I loved."

"Well, it's pretty much the same when we lose someone that we love, no matter what. Next time you have group, you can tell the lady that."

"I will," said the little girl.

A young teenage boy joined us. He said hello to the girl and to Woody and Katie. "I'm getting a dog," he said.

"That's good news," I replied. "When?"

He was slow to answer and never took his eyes off Woody and Katie, petting them and concentrating on their fur. "I gotta go live with my gramma. My mom is in this hospital and then I am going to live with my gramma."

"I'm sorry," I said, and truly meant it. "Is she going to get you a dog?"

He nodded his head. "She says that after I move in, we can go to the shelter and pick out a dog because the dogs at shelter have also lost someone that they love. She says we can help each other."

I felt a twinge of admiration for his enlightened grandmother who had said that beautiful thing to him.

Driving home from the children's festival I began to cry. This had been the one and only time that I left hospice with tears and a profound sense of sadness. There were, of course, other times I had felt very sad; like the time I felt deprived of a new friendship I would never explore; the time I felt bad for a tiny infant who never had a chance at life; and the time I felt angry at the unnecessary destruction of healthy Cocker Spaniels. But I always knew that the people I had met along the journey would move on, as I did, and find peace once again. Being with the children that night flooded me with a whole new range of emotions because I knew that those children's lives were being touched in a way in which they would never recover. They would move on too, of course, but their lives were changed forever.

But there was more than that. I also felt a deep, deep respect for the dedicated people who touch these lives every day, for the institution of hospice that fosters the concept of death with dignity, and an awe for their sense of purpose and resolve to continue despite bearing the burdens of broken lives and loves.

But there was still more than that. I cried with overwhelming love and gratitude to Woody and Katie for being the miracles of nature they are—the beauty in their spirits, the loyalty to people in trouble, and their devotion to the sick and dying. I felt pride and humbled at the series of circumstances that brought our lives together for a time so we could touch the lives of others.

And I felt empowered: strong and sure that the work we were doing was important work, essential and very, very good. And I knew that, once again, when the time has come for the healers in their white coats to come to terms with the finality of cancer and AIDS and hepatitis and heart disease and human mortality that it's time to send in the healers with fur coats.

It is time to send in the hospice hounds.

Afterword ⁓

I DID NOT SET OUT TO MAKE THIS A BOOK THAT served any specific cause. However, there was one theme that kept recurring, and to ignore it or dismiss it as coincidence when there is progress to be made would be a disservice to wonderful dogs and cats like Katie, Woody, Kelly, and Sable and all the others mentioned in this book.

My research turned up a tragic fact. The number one reason animals are given up at shelters is because the family is moving to a place where "no pets are allowed." For this reason, thousands of animals are killed in our nation's shelters every year.

We don't stand by and allow bias against race, religion, age, sex, or cultural differences, yet we allow bias against our best friends—friends who love us unconditionally and who visit the dying, cheer up little children, and so much more. They deserve to be protected against unfairness just like anyone else. But it is the guardians who must make it so.

Dogs need to be taken to school and taught good behavior just like children do. Dogs love to do homework! They love to please; they want to be an important part of our world. We must make them good citizens and teach them well. Only then will they be welcome in the places we live and we won't have to "put them away" or surrender them to shelters or abandon them.

The faces of the people in the rooms that we visited told the story. They love dogs. According to a 1999–2000 pet facts survey carried out by the American Animal Hospital Association, ninety-eight percent of surveyed dog owners freely admit to buying presents for their dogs at Christmas and birthdays. Yet we stand mute when told they cannot live with us.

Americans love and rejoice in their companion animals. There are so many ways to celebrate the wonderful relationships we enjoy with our dogs and cats. We must celebrate them all and then write about them! Write their stories. When your mother, father, or grandparents are dying, write their favorite animal stories. They have so many stories to tell. If not animal stories, then write their favorite recipes. Write their favorite songs. Give them a journal and write what they tell you. Write joyfully; write reverently. Write calmly and with wild abandon! Use the writing as therapy for both of you. Write the stories for future generations. And know that when someone is dying, their companion animals feel the pain and isolation, too. Talk to them, take them for car rides and long walks. Bring them to the grooming parlor, the vet, the trainer. Then relate in speech and writings the stories about how their dog reacted to new people and places and things. Do this so that your loved one can die knowing that someone truly does understand their beloved dog or cat almost as much as they do. Do this so they know that someone loves their companion animal, and will always love them, when they no longer can.

Michelle A. Rivera
Jupiter, Florida
December 14, 2000